Households of Faith

The rituals and relationships
that turn a home into a sacred space

Research commissioned by Lutheran Hour Ministries, St. Louis, Missouri
Research conducted by Barna Group, Ventura, California

Funding for this research was made possible by the generous support of Lutheran Hour Ministries. Barna Group was solely responsible for data collection, analysis and writing of the report.

Table of Contents

A Multi-Year Look at America's Faith

You are reading the second of three research reports from Barna, in partnership with Lutheran Hour Ministries. These studies seek to reveal how Americans are expressing their faith: from the conversations individuals have, to the influence of households on spiritual development, to the impact of Christians on the broader community. Join us as we discover both the private and the public ways faith continues to shape American life.

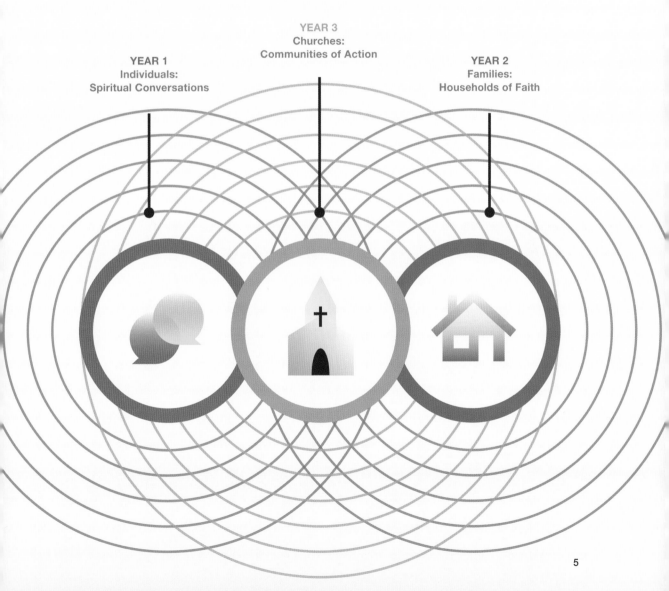

YEAR 3
Churches:
Communities of Action

YEAR 1
Individuals:
Spiritual Conversations

YEAR 2
Families:
Households of Faith

Preface

by Kurt S. Buchholz

President & CEO of Lutheran Hour Ministries

Recently I was in church on a Sunday morning and was surprised and delighted by what I saw up on the screens in the front of the church. They were displaying data and findings from *Spiritual Conversations in the Digital Age,* Lutheran Hour Ministries (LHM) and Barna Group's last study, which looked at how Christians' approach to sharing their faith has changed in the last 25 years.

I was most amazed to learn that the information on the screens that Sunday had only made it into the pastor's hands the previous night. This was a clear picture to me that when leaders are given clarity about the state of the world and the Church's mission within it, they don't hesitate to put that clarity into action. Our research with Barna, it turns out, is filling a great need in our churches—and leaders are not keeping it to themselves.

This reminds me of the importance of our daily work and ongoing mission at LHM: bringing Christ to the Nations, and the Nations to the Church. You see, we invested in careful research about the state of spiritual conversations because LHM is curious about how people talk about their faith and wants to equip and inspire Christians to have more fruitful discussions about these topics. Barna helped us do just that, and now we continue our partnership with a second round of cutting-edge research, *Households of Faith*.

Having explored the dynamics that affect how individuals share their faith, we wanted to broaden the scope to consider how faith is handed down and nurtured within households. The data pulls back the curtain and discovers powerful insights about how faith is being handled in practicing Christians' homes. For example, we have learned that:

- Faith experiences in youth affect Christians' beliefs and practices into adulthood.
- Faith formation and hospitality go hand in hand.
- Mothers' spiritual influence seems to be especially positive and enduring.
- Couple households, primarily made up of Boomers and Elders, are less interactive with extended households and community.
- Spiritually vibrant households share traits that can be nurtured within any household.

It's that last finding that has me particularly excited. The qualities of these vibrant households where faith is cultivated in a beautiful, lasting way are attainable for any household—no matter the size or makeup—which is good news for the cause of the gospel. Any spiritually dormant household can become, over time and with intention, a spiritually vibrant household of faith.

Having seen how careful thinking and strategic leadership in the area of spiritual conversations has already blessed local churches, I am confident that, by God's grace, the study you are about to read will lead to real life change for countless households. The reality is, the size and shape and complexity of households is shifting, but the role of the household in instilling and nurturing the Christian faith remains the same. Every church is filled with parents longing to raise their children in the faith, grandparents who want to leave a spiritual legacy, singles and empty nesters who want to grow in their faith—and help others grow as well! Here, in *Households of Faith*, you'll find powerful insights to help all of these groups establish the rituals and relationships that turn a home into a sacred space. I pray that church leaders, pastors and household members of every age and stage of life are as encouraged, challenged and enlightened as we have been.

At LHM, we are committed to seeing the Christian faith instilled and nurtured within vibrant households of faith. I invite you to read on and join us in this mission.

The size and shape and complexity of households is shifting, but the role of the household in instilling and nurturing the Christian faith remains the same

Introduction

Barna Group undertook this *Households of Faith* study to learn how practicing Christians' core relationships engage them in a thoughtful, transformative faith—the kind that holds up to and is passed down over time. Understanding such rituals and relationships is important because, as shown in *Spiritual Conversations in the Digital Age,* our first report in partnership with Lutheran Hour Ministries, most people today are reluctant to even *speak* about faith.[1] Less than one-quarter of American adults has a spiritual conversation once a month. More than half of people who claim no religion (55%) say they simply aren't interested in the topic. Concerns about coming off as angry, disrespectful or judgmental are main reasons people feel it can be inappropriate to discuss spiritual matters.

Compared to data collected in 1993, we see that Christians, too, have had a change of heart about spiritual conversations. Whether quoting scripture (59% in 1993 vs. 37% in 2017), telling the story of how they came to believe in Jesus (57% vs. 45%) or simply feeling a responsibility to share about their faith in the first place (89% vs. 64%), Christians are generally less vocal. Meanwhile, sacred dialogue seems to have moved into the more private spheres of life. For instance, Christians today are actually *more* likely to seek out opportunities to discuss faith (19% in 2017 vs. 11% in 1993), but they think this is best done within established relationships (47% vs. 37%). Their preferred spiritual conversation partners include close friends and family members, usually a spouse or child.

Sacred dialogue seems to have moved into the more private spheres of life

For the Church, some of these statistics are indicators of a decline in Christianity's public standing or of timidity among believers. But the *Spiritual Conversations in the Digital Age* study also underscored the power of intimacy in faith formation. People who report having a major life change as a result of a spiritual conversation usually note that this interaction occurred in person (73%), through multiple one-on-one conversations (42%) and with someone they knew well (88%).

With an awareness that Christianity has become more tense, complex or even hidden in public, we now turn the lens of our research toward how it is being nurtured and lived out in private—with the people who come and go from under Christians' roofs. This report is the product of a series of qualitative in-person interviews with various households and quantitative online surveys of 2,347 practicing Christians (including 448 with teens between the ages of 13–17), exploring the makeup of households and the ways in which they interact, spiritually and otherwise. At the heart of these surveys are our own guiding questions: What does faith look like on a day-to-day basis, in practicing Christians' most familiar relationships, personal environments or unobserved hours? With the help of churches, how might that everyday faith become vibrant and enduring?

> What does faith look like on a day-to-day basis, in practicing Christians' most familiar relationships, personal environments or unobserved hours?

The New Shape of American Households

Any study of U.S. practicing Christians should be assessed against the backdrop of U.S. adults as a whole. In this case, American households and family units have changed significantly in recent decades. We see this, for example, in Millennials' hesitancy to get married and have children, meaning many of these young adults share their living spaces with roommates, significant others or their parents.[2] A plummeting national divorce rate—down 18 percentage points between 2008 and 2016—has also been attributed to Millennials, though that could reflect instability in the economy as much as prudence in relationships;[3] if college and career are regarded as the precursor to commitment, those with lower levels of education and income are less likely to take a walk down the aisle. Some young adults may come around to starting families, whether or not they have a spouse; more than half of never-married women in their early 40s have birthed a child, up 6 percentage points from just a decade ago.[4] The post-recession economic climate, as well as growing racial diversity, have also given rise to more multi-generational living arrangements.[5]

As you can see, the sing-song premise that "first comes love, then comes marriage, then comes baby in the baby carriage" doesn't always apply—and if it does, it might take time. And money. As social historian and author Stephanie Coontz, says, "We're seeing a class divide not only between the haves and the have-nots, but between the I do's and the I do nots."[6] New economic realities persist into marriage partnerships too: Between 1960 and 2011, the share of married women who out-earn their husbands climbed from 6 percent to 24 percent.[7]

The forces that shape U.S. households (such as rates of marriage and divorce, living and housing costs, fertility patterns, education levels, societal values, geography and so on) are myriad and in flux. Though it's not explored in this particular study, we can assume the practicing Christian segment is more likely to hold to some traditional ideas about marriage and family that might curb a few of these domestic trends—but not entirely. As you'll see in the coming chapters, Christians and their households are navigating many of these same household changes and challenges.

An Invitation into Christians' Homes

The findings contained in this report are intended not only to shed light on households of faith, but to provide insights for leaders who disciple them. If a church is much more than a building, or if a congregation is ultimately the sum of its people and families, how can a ministry contribute to the health of households? In turn, how can each household contribute to the health of the Church?

This study reveals patterns, and at times clear principles, about spiritual development in the home. It also points to some groups of Christians who might struggle (or neglect) to create time for connective moments, if only for a season of life:

- Having children in a household is a spark for conversations and activities related to faith—or anything else, for that matter—while homes without minors have less give-and-take.
- Mothers surpass fathers (and most individuals) in multiple dimensions of closeness and faith formation, even when children are grown.
- Couple households, usually made up of older empty nesters, have more secluded lifestyles marked by regular, meaningful exchanges between spouses, and rarely anyone else.
- Young unmarried adults often live in roommate contexts, and though their households are extensive and hospitable, their spiritual interactions are more sporadic.

These are just some of the ways that age, relationship status, the presence of minors or the number of housemates all have great bearing on the frequency and diversity of spiritual interactions—but robust faith engagement as a household is, more than anything, a product of intention and decision. Much of our analysis rightly examines ages and stages, noting contextual differences and tendencies, but common threads suggest that anyone—regardless of their season or station in life—can nurture a spiritually vibrant household. The importance of fostering intimacy, sharing rituals and having fun with housemates—as well as friends and other non-family guests who become a part of one's extended household—cannot be overstated. Faith is stimulated by hospitality and formed in community.

The Proverbs proclaim, "A house is built by wisdom and becomes strong through good sense. Through knowledge its rooms are filled with all sorts of precious riches and valuables" (24:3–4). We present *Households of Faith* with the hope that it might impart fresh wisdom and understanding to produce spiritual vibrancy in followers of Christ, their homes and, ultimately, the family of God.

Much of our analysis rightly examines ages and stages, noting contextual differences and tendencies, but anyone can nurture a spiritually vibrant household

At a Glance

Generally active households are spiritually active households, and vice versa.

Shared meals, work and play are common in households that also carve out time for faith interactions.

Faith formation is connected to and increases with hospitality.

Households that regularly host non-family guests are more likely to talk about faith, pray or read the Bible together.

A majority of practicing Christians participates in spiritual conversations, prayer and Bible-reading with their household.

Beyond the home, church attendance is also a common group activity, behind only eating out in frequency.

Practicing Christians occupy many kinds of households, primarily as nuclear families or in roommate contexts.

For the most part, Christians also live with people of the same ethnic background and religious identity.

Faith heritage impacts Christians' beliefs and practices for the long term.

Christians need influences outside their family of origin or household to grow in both theology and tradition.

Overall, spouses are the primary relationship that Christians interact with and confide in.

Unmarried adults have a more diverse mix of people on whom they depend, though mothers top their list.

Couple households, primarily made up of Boomers and Elders, are fairly isolated.

The routines of these older Christians tend to orbit their spouse, and half do not regularly welcome guests.

Kids become a catalyst for any interaction, including faith-related ones.

Homes with minors have broader communities, busier schedules and more spiritual conversations.

Spiritually vibrant households are characterized by fun and quality time.

Games, singing, reading and sports are common group activities among households that Barna defines as Vibrant.

Fathers play a smaller role than mothers in terms of both presence and influence in their households.

Teenagers' siblings are equally as involved as their fathers in meeting emotional and spiritual needs.

An Introduction to the Spiritually Vibrant Household

One of the goals of this study was to learn from households that appear to be exceptionally engaged in communal and consistent faith expression in the home. Barna developed a custom metric that sorts households by reports of collective, frequent engagement in key behaviors: spiritual practices, spiritual conversations and hospitality. The result is four distinct profiles that indicate levels of spiritual vibrancy in the places practicing Christians call home.

To learn more about the traits of each household type and what sets them apart, refer to chapter five.

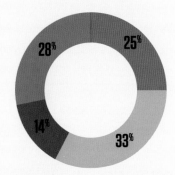

Distribution of the Spectrum of Spiritual Vibrancy

28% 25% 14% 33%

n=2,347 U.S. practicing Christian adults and teens, April 5–11, 2018.

● Vibrant

These households talk about God or faith together weekly, pray together every day or two, read the Bible together weekly and welcome non-family visitors at least several times a month.

One in four U.S. practicing Christians lives in a household that qualifies as Vibrant

● Devotional

These households talk about God or faith together weekly, pray together every day or two and read the Bible together weekly. They do not welcome non-family visitors at least several times a month.

One in three U.S. practicing Christians lives in a household that qualifies as Devotional

● Hospitable

These households welcome non-family visitors several times a month. They do not talk about God or faith together weekly, do not pray together every day or two and do not read the Bible together weekly. They might participate in some of these spiritual activities, but not all of them at this frequency.

About one in seven U.S. practicing Christians lives in a household that qualifies as Hospitable

● Dormant

These households do not talk about God or faith together weekly, do not pray together every day or two, do not read the Bible together weekly and do not welcome non-family visitors at least several times a month. They might participate in some of these spiritual activities, but not all of them at this frequency.

Over one-quarter of U.S. practicing Christians lives in a household that qualifies as Dormant

At Home with Christians

What makes a household? According to the U.S. Census Bureau, the term simply refers to "all the people who occupy a housing unit."[8] These people could be family members related by birth, marriage or adoption, as well as non-family such as boarders, foster children, wards, employees and so on. It's a fittingly vague definition, considering the evolving nature of American households, both at this moment and over time. There are not only multiple kinds of households in general—many of which do not fit a stereotypical nuclear family construct—but the average person will progress through various types of households during their lifetime. The diversity of household models is of particular interest to church leaders, as their congregants likely represent a range of living arrangements themselves, each with its own opportunities to form and be formed by the rituals and relationships therein.

For this study of practicing Christians, Barna categorized households based on how respondents describe their homes and housemates. The primary categories observed are: **nuclear family households** made up of two parents and their children (25% of the total sample); **roommate households** made up of unmarried adults who share a home (17%); **couple households** made up of spouses with no children at home (14%); **single-parent households** made up of one parent and their children (12%); and **multi-generational households** made up of at least three generations in the home or a grandparent raising a grandchild (12%). There is a small overlap between these last two categories. A smaller segment of **grown-up, or all-adult, nuclear family households** (5%), made up of two parents and their grown offspring, is described further on page 73.

Combinations of any of the above categories are included in "other" households. Though it comprises 17 percent of the sample, this "other" group is not often included in this report, as its miscellaneous compositions and circumstances make it difficult to analyze. Think of this segment as multiple small, untraditional households that do not have enough statistical significance to be included for comparison (examples include adults or teens living with siblings or relatives other than their parents, adults who are married and / or have children and also live with roommates and so on).

Distribution of Household Types in This Study

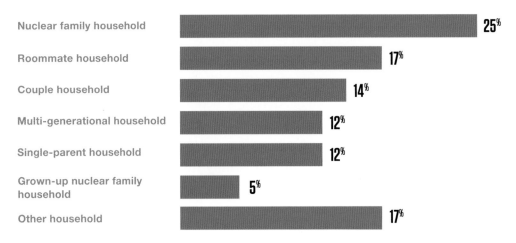

Nuclear family household	25%
Roommate household	17%
Couple household	14%
Multi-generational household	12%
Single-parent household	12%
Grown-up nuclear family household	5%
Other household	17%

Using various approaches to population estimates, Barna projects that between one in 10 and one in five practicing Christians live alone without anyone else in their home. Please see the Methodology in the Appendix for a detailed description of how and why the study focused on multi-person households, as well as profiles of the household types.

n=2,347 U.S. practicing Christian adults and teens, April 5–11, 2018. Total does not add up to 100 percent due to small overlap in single-parent and multi-generational groups.

The median size for nuclear and multi-generational households—the busiest homes examined in this survey—is four people. The average (mean) number of household members runs slightly larger for nuclear families, a third of which (33%) has two kids at home. Roommate setups are typically quite small; half (51%) refer to just two people sharing a space. Single-parent homes are also more intimate, usually including a mom or dad with just one (21%) or two (33%) children. Couple households, by definition, contain only two people.

Though they are a growing group, *individuals living by themselves are excluded from this study altogether*. That's not to dismiss the valuable spiritual communities and practices that these solo residents take part in both inside and outside their home—indeed, their presence is implied among regular visitors to other households, who often play a crucial role in faith formation. This sample, however, is not designed to be representative of all household types in the U.S.—more than a quarter of which, census data tells us, are made up of one person.[9] Instead, the goal of this study is to observe interactions among practicing Christians who live together and how faith is experienced and transmitted among them. Thus, households of a single person did not qualify for participation.

The goal of this study is to observe interactions among practicing Christians who live together and how faith is being transmitted among them

Traits of Respondents & Households

By offering a glimpse of the domestic experiences of practicing Christians today, this report aims to help churches better reflect and disciple a vast array of family and household types. In the process, it also naturally speaks to different seasons of life and generational experiences. Among this sample, couple households are dominated by Boomers (59%), presumably because a large proportion of these adults is now empty-nesting. Similarly, this is also the type of household that sees the most Elders (22%). Gen X is the adult generation usually found in a nuclear family scenario; three in 10 respondents in this category (30%) belong to this generation—still well ahead of the percentage of Millennials in this category (18%). Millennials, meanwhile, are most represented among roommate households; 39 percent of this category is made up of these young adults. Barna's survey also includes Christian teens, members of the leading edge of Gen Z. These young respondents make up half of the study's nuclear families (49%) and more than a fifth of single-parent households (22%).

As you can see, many Millennials live in household structures that aren't defined by spouses and children, and do so longer than adult generations before them. Further, Barna data predicts Gen Z may be following suit, with marriage and family ranking fairly low on their present list of priorities.[10]

Household Type, by Generation

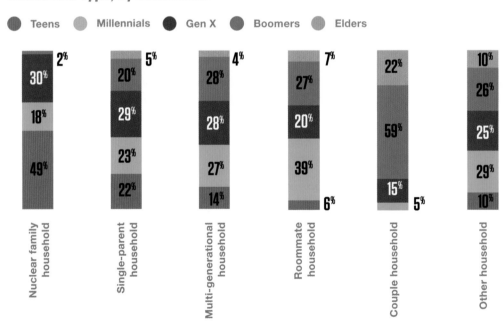

● Teens ● Millennials ● Gen X ● Boomers ● Elders

Nuclear family household: 2%, 30%, 18%, 49%
Single-parent household: 5%, 20%, 29%, 23%, 22%
Multi-generational household: 4%, 28%, 28%, 27%, 14%
Roommate household: 7%, 27%, 20%, 39%, 6%
Couple household: 22%, 59%, 15%, 5%
Other household: 10%, 26%, 25%, 29%, 10%

n=2,347 U.S. practicing Christian adults and teens, April 5–11, 2018.

Considering this, churches that want to understand and serve teens and young adults—a skeptical group with a higher tendency to drop out of church—should focus first on true *household* ministry, not just family ministry.

If thinking of congregations as collections of households, it's important to consider how these structures also vary in minority or multi-ethnic contexts. White respondents are more likely to have couples-only residences (19% vs. 6% of non-white respondents). Non-white households are usually slightly bigger than that of white respondents, with Hispanic households being the largest. Minorities more often live in a single-parent (19% vs. 9% of white respondents) or roommate context (23% vs. 14%). For the most part (85%), households are made up of occupants who all share the same ethnic backgrounds, so churches hoping to cultivate integrated, diverse faith communities should note the reality that homogeneity starts in our homes.

High income is associated with nuclear families, and the lowest incomes are reported among roommate households, followed by single-parent homes. It shouldn't be automatically assumed, however, that nuclear families are financially comfortable. Their salaries must also stretch to accommodate, on average, a greater number of residents. Respondents of an ethnic minority typically report lower income; one in five non-white practicing Christians in this study (20%) makes less than $20,000 annually.

This study's sample is predominantly Protestant, though about a third of the practicing Christians surveyed (34%) identifies as Catholic, a group that sees similar representation across household types. According to Barna's theolographics (see the glossary in the Appendix for all definitions), similar proportions across all households qualify as nominal Christians. Evangelicals are less common, but appear most in the "other" and couple households.

Churches that want to understand and serve teens and young adults should focus first on true household ministry, not just family ministry

Types of Neighborhoods Households Occupy

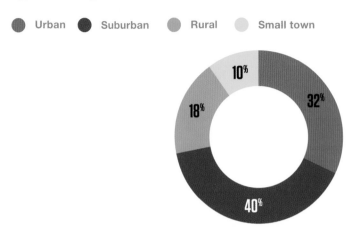

● Urban ● Suburban ● Rural ● Small town

32%
40%
18%
10%

n=2,347 U.S. practicing Christian adults and teens, April 5–11, 2018.

As we delve into household experiences in the following pages, imagine either suburban neighborhoods (40%) or urban streets (32%). Practicing Christians living in rural areas (18%) or small towns (10%) make up a minority of the sample.

For a more extensive breakdown of the demographics and dynamics of each household type, refer to the profiles in the Appendix of this report.

Extended Households

A cornerstone of the concept for this study is that household dynamics are not only defined by occupants and family members, but by the people we invite (or don't invite) into our homes and routines. This study refers to these familiar faces as extended household members. Many practicing Christian respondents regularly host visitors at least several times a month. These guests—usually relatives (69%), but also close friends, neighbors, significant others, exes, caregivers and more—have a degree of influence on residents.

Still, two in five respondents (40%) say that nobody comes to spend time with them or other household members frequently. That percentage is highest among couple households, half of which (49%) don't have guests on a regular basis. When these couples do have company, it's usually their own adult children (29%) or perhaps also their grandchildren (23%). As mentioned above, couples in this sample who live alone are typically older, and this report consistently reveals them to be very family-centric—and also concerningly isolated—in this stage of life. In all other households, the most common type of guest is an intimate friend (22%), followed by siblings (13%), neighbors (11%), mothers (10%) or other relatives (10%).

Overall, statistical modeling reveals that one's generation and whether they have kids at home are the top predictors of how extensive an extended household may become. Millennials—though still less likely to be married, or living with or raising children themselves—are the generation most likely to have people in their home multiple times a month, perhaps because so many are in roommate contexts or are embracing a fairly social season of life as they focus on career, dating and friendships. Millennials also see a lot of value in opening their homes to others; a separate Barna study shows that one in five Millennials (21%)—more than any other age group—believes being hospitable is the best way to express generosity.[11]

Households with children tend to become hubs of meaningful social (and, as we'll see, spiritual) activities that transcend family bonds alone. Roughly one-quarter of homes with minors present (26% vs. 18% of others) consistently receives visits from friends. We've heard "it takes a village" to raise children, and the data seem to bear this proverb out—or at least suggest that raising children provides plenty of opportunities to get the village together.

Two in five respondents say that nobody comes to spend time with them or other household members frequently

"No One Comes to My Home on a Regular Basis"

● Couple household   ● Nuclear family household   ● Multi-generational household

● Roommate household   ● Single-parent household   ● Other

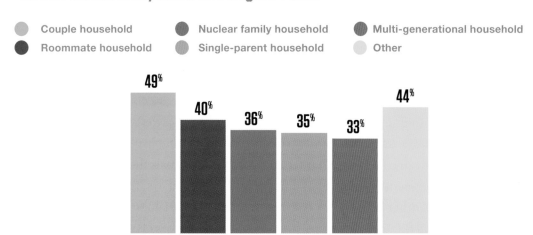

Top 5 Frequent Visitors for Each Type of Household

	Nuclear family household	Single-parent household	Multi-generational household	Roommate household	Couple household	Other household
1	A close friend 26%	A close friend 25%	A close friend 25%	A close friend 26%	Adult child 29%	A close friend 20%
2	Sibling 15%	Sibling 19%	Sibling 17%	Sibling 15%	Grandchild 23%	Sibling 13%
3	Mother 14%	Mother 14%	Neighbor 17%	Neighbor 11%	A close friend 15%	Mother 12%
4	Grandparent 13%	Neighbor 12%	Other relative 11%	Boyfriend or girlfriend 9%	Son- / daughter-in-law 14%	Other relative 12%
5	Neighbor 10%	Child's close friend 11%	Grandchild 10%	Mother 8%	Neighbor 10%	Neighbor 10%

n=2,347 U.S. practicing Christian adults and teens, April 5–11, 2018.

Throughout this study, we see that welcoming households—typically, households that are larger and / or with children present—are prone to foster spiritual development, especially when non-family guests are the norm. On a similar note, a sense of responsibility to tell others about one's Christian beliefs is common among those who have regular guests; 50 percent of this hospitable segment hold this belief (vs. 44% of those who don't have frequent visitors). This is *not* to suggest people have guests in order to evangelize; rather, these characteristics may be associated with those who, for example, are more candid and open with others or who perhaps try to emulate the New Testament Church values of fellowship and breaking bread (Acts 2:42). Generally, faith formation is connected to and increases with a spirit of hospitality.

Faith formation is connected to and increases with a spirit of hospitality

Where Two or More Are Gathered ...

Hospitality is the heart of Christian households

Practicing Christians who have regular visitors in their homes are more likely to forge deep, meaningful relationships both within and outside of their homes.

● Households with regular visitors   ● Households without regular visitors

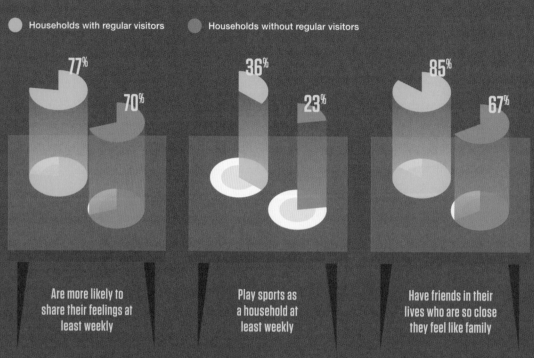

77% / **70%**
Are more likely to share their feelings at least weekly

36% / **23%**
Play sports as a household at least weekly

85% / **67%**
Have friends in their lives who are so close they feel like family

What happens when these close friends get together?

% among those who have regular visitors

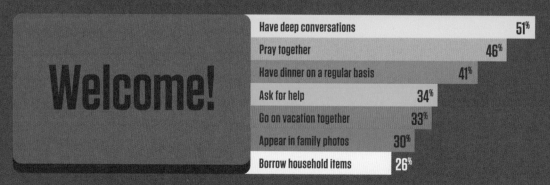

Welcome!

Have deep conversations	51%
Pray together	46%
Have dinner on a regular basis	41%
Ask for help	34%
Go on vacation together	33%
Appear in family photos	30%
Borrow household items	26%

The More the Merrier

Households where minors are present are more likely to have regular visitors

- Households with minors at home
- Households without minors at home

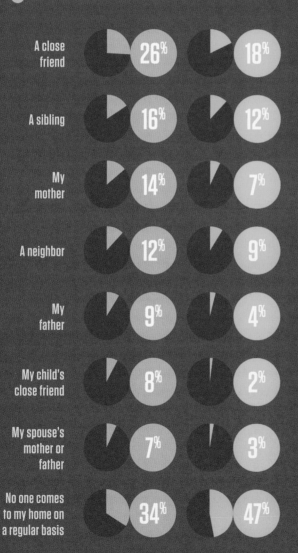

	With minors	Without minors
A close friend	26%	18%
A sibling	16%	12%
My mother	14%	7%
A neighbor	12%	9%
My father	9%	4%
My child's close friend	8%	2%
My spouse's mother or father	7%	3%
No one comes to my home on a regular basis	34%	47%

Do Not Disturb

Four in 10 practicing Christian households do not regularly host visitors. Which households are least likely to host visitors? Couple households. Nearly half admit they don't have people over very often.

49% Couple households

39% Roommate households

36% Nuclear family households

35% Single-parent households

33% Multi-generational households

n=2,347 U.S. practicing Christian adult and teens, April 5-11, 2018.

Starting Small

A Q&A with Bianca Robinson Howard

 What are practical, realistic approaches for households to organize their days and interactions in a way that prioritizes shared spiritual moments and everyday liturgies?

> "That is spiritual practice: being intentional in those moments that are already in our routines."

The environment doesn't have to be perfect. Take small moments to do small things: eating together, reading scripture, sharing, praying in the car, showing random acts of kindness. That is spiritual practice: being intentional in those moments that are already in our routines.

My husband and I began a routine back in our engagement where, every Thursday, we sat down for a devotion and prayer, and we would talk about our budget. That started as our habit going into the wedding, and we still meet on Thursday nights for prayer and devotion. I know we're in a hustle-and-bustle society, but I hope that this will carry on when our kids are here, that we take that time as a family, even if it's once a week.

In my experience, you can definitely see the difference when the heads of household, whether it's both parents or a single mom or dad, are taking the lead. It is very clear in children, youth and family ministry. You see the ones who make sure their kids are there on Sundays. Nowadays, not a lot of kids carry Bibles; well, I see a couple 7- and 8-year-olds who bring their Bibles every week. That says something. Something's happening at home, where their mom is like, "Grab your Bible." I've commended them for that—or just for the fact that the child

Reverend Bianca Robinson Howard

Children & Youth Pastor

Bianca has a degree in broadcast journalism from Valdosta State University, an MDiv from Howard University School of Divinity and ThM from Princeton Theological Seminary (PTS). She is currently an associate pastor and the full-time children and youth pastor at Zion Baptist Church in Marietta, Georgia. Bianca also has served as a chaplain for Emory University Hospital, a blogger and mentor for Baptist Women in Ministry, a staff member for the Academy of Preachers and a representative for the PTS Alumni Association Executive Council. Her missions experience has taken her to India, throughout Africa, Costa Rica and Europe. She is in the process of authoring her first book, addressing the fundamentals of a successful children & youth ministry in the black church setting.

even has a Bible! When parents are starting that process early, the kids will follow.

How can the Church help moms and dads share the crucial responsibilities of faith formation?

Whether it's the dad or the mom, if somebody is taking that spiritual lead, I think it will still help the child, despite what is going on and how their household is structured. I'm in a predominantly African American church within an African American community, and we have more single moms. They still bring their family to church. They're still making spirituality a priority, and you see the difference in the kids.

One thing we do is try to put men in front of our boys to help them in Bible study, Sunday school classes or youth groups, so they can have a role model. They have somebody they feel like they can talk to. I know our pastor has been a huge advocate of focusing on men in our church. It started with his intentionality, and it began to change the landscape of the church. We got more men volunteering. We also have mentoring groups. That's something we really push with men, but for the women and girls as well, if they need a little bit of extra support. Moms can't do everything.

How can church leaders be more considerate of the needs in their congregation and create multi-generational, multi-household connections?

If you wonder why people don't show up at church all the time, try to find out exactly what is going on with them, don't just assume and pass judgment. Give them a call. In our church, the deacons are connected by letters of the alphabet to our families. For example, there is a deacon that's in charge of checking in with the families whose last name starts with an H. We also have a lot of people who like to give to kids who can't go to camp, maybe empty nesters with a little extra money who can reach out to help another family do something.

It starts with recognizing the blind spots, being aware of the plight of society right now and what reality is. I know that's one thing I have to do: Have that extra grace and pray, "Lord, open my eyes to what is going on in my congregation, so I can be more sensitive and more understanding." It's getting out of that bubble of our own lives.

How can households also get out of their bubbles, intentionally cultivating an environment of diversity in their homes and routines?

Again, it starts with the adults and trickles down to the kids. I think sometimes we hide from these conversations because we're afraid of going that deep with kids. But, actually, it's probably the best time to talk about it, because they don't really have that fear of the other.

What are guardians and caregivers exposing children to outside of their own environment? In a white family, are they teaching kids about black history, going to black history museums or watching shows that have all black casts? Same with black households. Are they looking to try to learn about a different culture? It's important to stay open, or to be welcoming if somebody brings a white friend to church. If the kids are learning something related to race in school, maybe ask them, "Hey, what are you learning about that?" If you have friends of another race, make them welcome in your home. Sometimes the fear of the different or unknown keeps us in our pockets, and we've got to get out and get to know each other and celebrate one another. ●

"What are guardians and caregivers exposing children to outside of their own environment?"

Most households have a shared faith

 77% share a faith with the members of their household

 26% have a household member who does not share their faith

The majority of practicing Christians inherited their faith from someone in their household of origin

However, a significant minority admits they are still Christians despite the faith they grew up with.

 59%
Yes, someone passed their faith down to me

 23%
I'm a Christian despite the sort of Christianity I saw in my household growing up

 15%
No, my Christianity as an adult is not because of a person in my childhood household

 11%
Yes, someone explored faith at the same time I did

 2%
Other

n=1,116 U.S. practicing Christian adults who say they became a Christian after birth, April 5-11, 2018.

Mothers had the strongest faith impact on most respondents

 **68%** Mother

 46% Father

 37% Grand-parent

 16% Non-relative

 14% Friend

 10% Another relative

9% Sibling

- A family member was a negative example of faith
- A family member passed faith down
- A family member explored faith at the same time I did
- No family faith experience

Perhaps surprisingly, those who grew up without a faith—or clung to their faith despite a negative childhood experience of faith—have stronger theological convictions than those who inherited their faith

44% 29% 25% 52%

If a person is generally good, or does enough good things for others, they can earn a place in heaven (disagree strongly)

44% 30% 32% 50%

The devil, or Satan, is not a living being but is a symbol of evil (disagree strongly)

54% 58% 48% 41%

I have a responsibility to tell other people my religious belief (agree strongly)

55% 36% 40% 60%

When he lived on earth, Jesus Christ was human and committed sins, like other people (disagree strongly)

75% 60% 62% 82%

When you die you will go to heaven because you have confessed your sins and trust in Jesus Christ as your savior

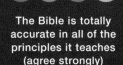

75% 65% 60% 60%

The Bible is totally accurate in all of the principles it teaches (agree strongly)

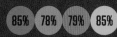

85% 78% 79% 85%

God is the all-powerful, all-knowing, perfect creator of the universe who rules the world today

n=1,116 U.S. practicing Christian adults who say they became a Christian after birth, April 5-11, 2018.

Faith Heritage & Histories

2

A majority of practicing Christians tells Barna they became Christians long before adulthood, usually before they were 12 years old (68%). This is true regardless of the type of household practicing Christians now occupy—in fact, there are no significant variations in faith heritage when focusing on respondents by household type.

The idea of beliefs that transcend generations is beautiful, but is it also beneficial? That is, does an "inherited" religious identity contribute to the maturation and flourishing of the individual and their faith in the long run? How does this experience compare with that of people who come to Christianity on their own, without positive faith influences in childhood or later in life?

Before we look at the specific ways that households presently nurture faith, this chapter will offer a retrospective of practicing Christian adults' faith heritages and histories. (As teens are in a formative stage of life and many are still living with their families of origin, they are excluded from some of the more reflective questions related to the spiritual experiences and influences of their upbringing.)

A majority
of practicing
Christians
tells Barna
they became
Christians long
before adulthood

A Shared Faith in Childhood

For most practicing Christian adults, the early, formative days of discipleship occur in their family of origin, usually because Christianity was "passed down" to them by a particular relative (59%), though sometimes another family member was exploring faith around the same time as the respondent (11%). More than half of those who report growing up in the faith (57%) say they were Christian at the time of their birth, a response that is revealing either of their theology or of how extensively Christianity permeated their upbringing.

Over a third of respondents came to faith for reasons other than a positive interaction in their upbringing, including one in four (23%) who says it occurred in spite of a negative example of Christianity in the home. Typically, individuals without strong family roots in the religion say they became Christians later in their youth or, as is the case for 55 percent of this group, during adulthood.

Respondents could select all Christian heritage scenarios that applied, and we find that a variety of family-of-origin experiences overlap. For example, some people who say Christianity was passed down to them also say someone else explored faith at the same time (48%)

Faith Experiences with Families of Origin

Would you say you are a Christian as an adult because of a person you grew up with in your household? Check all that apply.

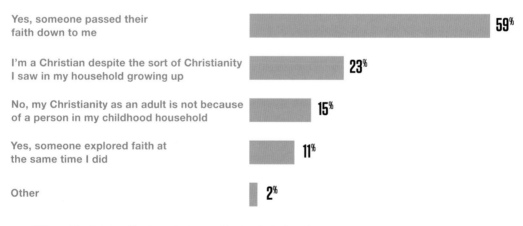

Yes, someone passed their faith down to me — **59%**

I'm a Christian despite the sort of Christianity I saw in my household growing up — **23%**

No, my Christianity as an adult is not because of a person in my childhood household — **15%**

Yes, someone explored faith at the same time I did — **11%**

Other — **2%**

n=1,116 U.S. practicing Christian adults who say they became a Christian after birth, April 5–11, 2018.

or that they had a negative example of Christianity in their household while growing up (17%). As you can see, inheriting faith is a common experience among respondents, but it does not eliminate the possibility of simultaneous experiences—even bad ones—with Christianity.

Practicing Christians most often credit their parents as the individuals who helped impart faith to them. In this and other responses throughout the report, it appears that spiritual development in the home is somewhat of a matriarchy. Two-thirds (68%) say they were most influenced by the Christian model of their mothers, compared to less than half (46%) who point to their fathers. More than a third (37%) looks back further into their lineage, to the spiritual influence of their grandparents, usually a grandmother.

Whose Faith Influenced You?

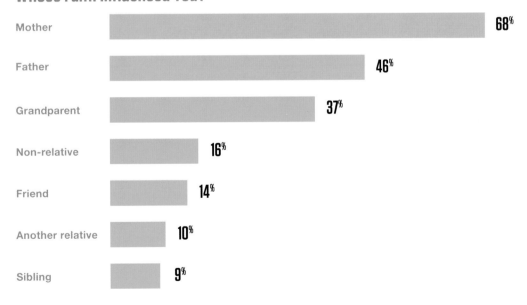

Mother	68%
Father	46%
Grandparent	37%
Non-relative	16%
Friend	14%
Another relative	10%
Sibling	9%

n=725 U.S. practicing Christian adults who grew up with someone who influenced their faith and who did not inherit their faith from birth. April 5–11, 2018.

Spiritual Upbringing Impacts Theology

A person's experience with Christianity while growing up does seem linked to their belief system even into adulthood, but a strong Christian heritage does not automatically equate to a strong Christian faith. Rather, taking ownership of one's beliefs or finding rich community may be required to build upon—or overcome—the spiritual experiences of one's upbringing.

Respondents who say someone passed Christianity down to them (40%) are actually more likely to hold a nominal faith, which is not characterized by a personal commitment to faith in Jesus (compared to 30% who had a negative Christian model in their upbringing and 21% of those who had no Christian influence in their upbringing). Their theology also tends to be less grounded in some of the traditional tenets of Christianity. They more often think of Satan as merely symbolic (54% agree strongly + somewhat) and 64 percent agree at least somewhat that people go to heaven if they are generally good. Fewer people in this group view God as the creator and ruler of the universe (79%) or affirm that they will go to heaven because of belief in Jesus' forgiveness (62%).

At the same time, those with a "family tree faith" are open and expressive. Whether they have a cursory or serious connection to Christianity as an adult, they are more likely to have spiritual conversations in their current households—environments which they describe as "peaceful" and "safe" and indicate are quite welcoming: Six in 10 (61%) regularly practice hospitality, compared to half of the respondents who did not carry Christianity with them from their upbringing (50%). It's possible that people who became Christians very young within a family context continue to model a lifestyle built around community and traditions.

Those whose Christian faith was absent or not positively nurtured in their families of origin could have a harder time establishing spiritual rituals and community in their current households. But though

An Unlikely Faith

A Profile of Respondents Who Grew up with Negative Examples of Christianity

What causes an adult who might be disillusioned with the Church and Christianity to stick with or come back to the faith? This is a question church leaders and many parents might ask, particularly as recent years have seen an uptick in the number of adults who become "church dropouts." New Barna data shows that, since 2011, the percentage of 18–to–29-year-olds who dropped out of the Church and / or their faith has increased from 59 percent to 64 percent.[12] Additionally, our Gen Z study reports that atheism is more likely among today's teens than any other generation.[13] In seeking some answers, it might be helpful to observe the group of practicing Christian adult respondents in this study who say they have come by a deep faith (usually in their teen years or early 20s) in spite of the fact that they had negative—or, at the least, mixed—feelings about the way Christianity was presented to them in their youth. In qualitative interviews, individuals who fit this category described "starting over" or "zig-zagging" in their faith practice over time. The quantitative studies help track that meandering spiritual journey.

The responses of this segment point to some estrangement in family units—and the problem seems most to lie with their parents.

Though they still note fathers and mothers as Christian presences from their upbringing, this group is more likely to name siblings, grandparents, other relatives and close friends as important spiritual figures in their youth. As adults, Christians with negative spiritual upbringings are consistently less likely than those with other heritages to identify their mothers or fathers as individuals who set a Christian example, taught them about God or encouraged church attendance. Their parents also less often come up as sources of help for other needs, like advice, sympathy or money. Just over half in this faith heritage group, which tends to be represented by Millennials and Gen X, say they continue any unique Christian traditions they learned from their family of origin, compared to two-thirds of those who positively identified with their childhood faith and three-quarters of those who explored faith with someone else in their youth. There are other signs of continued strain even in their current households; when describing their home environments, which are less interactive on several counts, the word "tense" pops up more.

For adults with this complicated faith heritage, regular activities, sensitive discussions or mere texts and phone calls with their immediate

their religious experience may appear less communal or instinctual, it is still thoughtful and assured. Consider that those who say their faith exists despite negative Christian examples in their family of origin are the group most certain of the inerrancy of scripture (94% agree strongly + somewhat), or that those whose Christianity is not linked to their upbringing at all are most convinced of salvation through belief in Jesus Christ (82%). It's possible that reacting against a negative or inconsistent model of faith prompts one to investigate and cling to these tenets. What these adults lack in religious legacy, they may find in devotion and discipleship. The roots of their faith are often younger, but they are well-tended.

One way or another, Christians need outside influences for robust faith formation. Adults whose upbringing did not plant them in meaningful Christian teachings or traditions might grow in community with their extended households. Meanwhile, adults with a long-held Christian identity might look to resources and voices beyond their family of origin to re-examine or strengthen their beliefs.

family of origin are rare. But there are still signs that these Christians are rooted in loving community, even if they are generally distant from their parents or siblings. If married, they prefer to sort out their faith views and practices with a partner; in fact, they are one of the rare groups who says a spouse even teaches them about traditions (perhaps because they are unlikely to feel attached to or warm toward any from their childhood, or because their spouse first drew them toward or back into a positive faith). They are also more likely than those with other faith backgrounds to report having multiple friends who feel like family.

These facts, as well as evidence of their strong commitment to scripture and other tenets of faith, give an impression of adults who have found refuge and stability—perhaps for the first time—in a faith and community that they chose and cultivated on their own. To them, Christianity isn't an heirloom; it's an anchor.

A Theology of Hospitality

A Q&A with Sandra Van Opstal

How should church teams account for a variety of household structures as they put together ministries and programs to reach families and individuals?

The first thing I think of is how we understand and view child care in the role of the ministries, especially in small groups. The small group structure is integral to the church experience. But you can't assume, for example, that people can have a sitter come and stay with the kids. In an economically diverse congregation, that could be a financial burden for some. In our church, the small groups that have been successful are ones that have provided child care within the small group setting for the families that needed it. We have a small group that meets in our house, and it's made up of young married couples, families with kids, single people who are not married and don't have kids, single parents. Because the small group is being held in a home where the children are being taken care of on the premises, it makes people in any of those situations feel welcome in that space. Especially for single moms or dads, they know they can physically be in the same place with their children, but also be in community with other adults. We actually have youth from the church watch the kids, and each different age group forms their own community. We've found it increases the level of commitment people have to the church overall. When they go on Sunday, the children also have connection to one another. They have a place of

Sandra Maria Van Opstal

Author, preacher, liturgist

Sandra is a second-generation Latina, pastors at Grace and Peace Church and lives on the west side of Chicago with her husband and two boys. She is a preacher, liturgist and activist reimagining the intersection of worship and justice. Sandra served with Urbana Missions Conference, Chicago Urban Program and Latino National Leadership Team (LaFe) of InterVarsity. Sandra's influence has also reached many others through preaching globally on topics such as worship and formation, justice, racial identity and reconciliation. Sandra is a board member for the Christian Community Development Association and holds a MDiv from Trinity Evangelical Divinity School. Her most recent books include *Still Evangelical* and *The Next Worship*.

belonging outside of Sunday as an entire family unit, and it makes for an easier transition from one affinity community to the next affinity community within the church.

Knowing that congregations are collections of households, and most practicing Christian households only live with people who share the same background, how can church leaders provide opportunities for inclusivity and integration in their church communities?

Whatever church leaders want to see, they have to model it for their congregants. Leaders have to model it and share about what they're experiencing, the good and the bad. And then leaders have to intentionally design worship practices that form disciples who care about the world around them. The practice of worship, which includes the preaching, should form disciples who see Jesus' heart for hospitality, solidarity, mutuality. But if we sing songs only about ourselves and God, and we close our eyes, and leaders say things to the congregation like, "Ignore everybody else in the room, it's just you and God, just have a moment," then we will never create disciples who go to the uncomfortable places of being in a relationship with people who are not like them. If the altar call is an invitation to be in a personal and private relationship with an individual God, just you and him, and not an invitation to a people or to a purpose, then we will never create disciples who go to the uncomfortable places of being in a relationship with people who are not like them. That is not an invitation that prepares you for the messiness and the disruption of cross-cultural, socioeconomically diverse relationships. The invitation is to be a part of this movement that God is creating in his people, to be pointers to his kingdom, to disrupt the order of the world around you so that people can see God's goodness and glory, to push against evil in the world, to stand up for peace, to love those who are unloved. We need a corrective to our Western theology—the idea that "all of it is about you"—that has infiltrated not only our preaching, but our worship practices.

> "Whatever church leaders want to see, they have to model it for their congregants."

What are some practical ways that you might encourage church leaders and lay people to practice hospitality by welcoming immigrants and refugees into their households and extended households?

Without immigrants and refugees and newcomers to our country, the American Church will dwindle. Just based off population growth, migration patterns and openness to spirituality and faith, the future of the Church in America is immigrants and people of color. Most of them are Bible-reading, passionate Christians whose faith has survived persecution, poverty, famine, oppression. They're bringing with them a level of faith in a God who sustains you that white American Christians could never understand.

Anybody who has an extra bed or an extra room could become a foster parent, receive a detained child or partner with a family. If you have space in your home, you should be asking yourself, why is it not occupied by someone who is in need? If you're a leader in a large church that's majority white and you don't have a lot of connections with ethnic minorities, start with the people you have on staff—if you don't know the stories of people working in your building, why have you not asked? I know a lot of churches have a pre-school that serves the neighborhood, and it might be of a different demographic than the church body—what have you done to have some kind of mutual relationship with them? Are there jobs that people in your church could provide for immigrants?

We can partner with immigrant churches or minority churches doing fantastic work in our communities and just say, "Hey, how can we be of help to you?" Then ask, "Is there anything you can help us with?" to have mutuality and reciprocity in our relationships. We can all work with organizations that are looking for churches and homes to house children who are in transition and waiting for sponsors. We can march together, we can pray together, we can fast together. There are a lot of practical things we can do, but it will require some proximity and some relationship, and if it's not already woven into the structure of the church, your family or your church community will have to find ways to do that. ●

"If you have space in your home, you should be asking yourself, why is it not occupied by someone who is in need?"

A Shared Faith in Adulthood

Whatever their experience with Christianity in their childhood home, most respondents across all of the household types now share the same faith as at least one other person who either lives under their

Mutual Faith Across Household Types

% of respondents in these household types who say they have anybody in their household or extended household who ...

● Shares the same faith totally or with few exceptions

● Says we have the same faith but has some different beliefs

● Doesn't have my faith

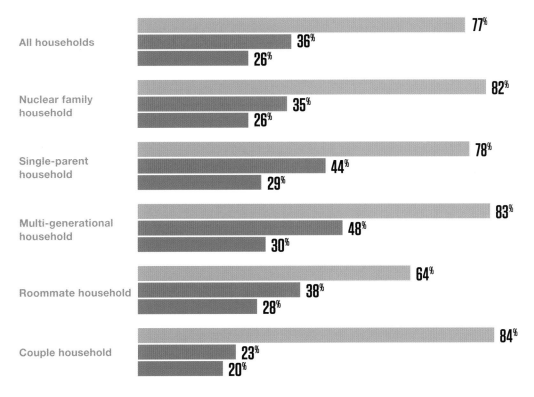

All households
- 77%
- 36%
- 26%

Nuclear family household
- 82%
- 35%
- 26%

Single-parent household
- 78%
- 44%
- 29%

Multi-generational household
- 83%
- 48%
- 30%

Roommate household
- 64%
- 38%
- 28%

Couple household
- 84%
- 23%
- 20%

n=1,899 U.S. practicing Christian adults, April 5–11, 2018. Respondents were only shown relationship types they live with or who visit them regularly in their home.

roof or regularly visits. Nearly three-quarters (77%) indicate sharing the same faith "either totally or with few exceptions" with a Christian in their household or extended household. One-third (36%) points to a household relationship with a Christian who has some significant differences in beliefs. A full quarter of respondents (26%), however, regularly shares space with someone who does not claim the same faith at all. A lack of religious overlap occurs more in multi-generational and roommate households.

Controlling for other factors, Boomers and Elders are the generations of practicing Christians most likely to hold the same faith as someone in their household or extended household. This checks out, given a general decrease in practicing faith among younger generations, as well as the fact that many older adults are living in couple contexts, in which three-quarters of respondents (76%) indicate their spouse is also a Christian.

The Role of Doubt in Faith Formation

by Rev. Dr. Jason Broge

"Does God really listen to our prayers?" "Do you really believe your Christian denomination is right and all others are wrong?" "Is Jesus really the only way to heaven?" "If God is loving, would he really send anyone to hell?" "I'm not so sure that God really created everything in just seven days."

The question can come in many forms; sometimes it isn't even a question, just an expression of doubt. For many Christians, there are few things scarier than being cornered by someone in your household who is struggling with some fundamental doubt about the faith. This fear is likely even more acute for parents who, as this report demonstrates (page 109), are often the first people children will bring their questions to. As Christians, we have this innate desire to protect kids from religious doubts in the hope that this will keep them within the walls of the kingdom. Yet research suggests that our desire to protect people from doubt may do more harm than good. Studies show doubt is an important part of the process in forming a healthy religious identity. As one researcher put it, "If a genuine and vibrant identity cannot emerge without exploration and doubt is linked to this criteria, then doubt of any kind ... appears to be related to healthy psychological development."[14]

At first glance, this seems counterintuitive to many people. Part of the problem stems from how we define doubt. Within the Church,

Rev. Dr. Jason Broge

Rev. Dr. Jason Broge is the associate director of design and development for Lutheran Hour Ministries. Jason served as a teacher for a number of years before becoming a pastor. After obtaining his PhD in education, he went on to serve as the director of curriculum design and development for Concordia Seminary.

> "Doubt, by its very nature, leads to both a stronger belief in something and unbelief in something else."

doubt is often seen as synonymous with unbelief. Yet for the purposes of research into human growth and development, doubt is distinct from unbelief. Doubt is a hesitation, a temporary divide in thought created "by the collision of evidence with prior belief, or one belief with another."[15] It is the attempt to resolve a mental disequilibrium "by pushing some ideas toward more certainty" over other ideas.[16] Unbelief, on the other hand, is an outright rejection of a belief or idea, a "resolute state of mind involving a definitive conviction of falsity regarding an issue."[17] Religious doubt can lead to unbelief, but it does not *have* to lead to unbelief. Doubt, by its very nature, leads to both a stronger belief in something and unbelief in something else.

Therefore, the question is not whether doubt will lead to unbelief, but which beliefs will be strengthened and which beliefs will be rejected. Doubt can lead to a strengthening of one's beliefs that Jesus is the only way to heaven even as it pushes one away from a pluralistic view of the road to heaven.

But what if it doesn't?

That "what if?" is the fear that keeps Christian parents from engaging in spiritual conversations about doubts with their children. The problem is these doubts don't go away. Doubt cannot be avoided; it is a natural part of human development. Research into human growth and development demonstrates that doubt is a key process a person goes through to confirm and take ownership of their identity. It occurs in all spheres of life, from work and family to social and religious realms. The period of time that defines how well a person will be able to handle the doubts life will continually throw at them is right around ages 18 to 24.[18] This is the time of life when the individual is transitioning from adolescence into young adulthood, transitioning from a time when decisions were being made by others (parents, school, church) to being made by self. The doubts come from all angles of life, not just the spiritual realm: *Do I really want to go to college? Am I just a Republican / Democrat because my parents are? What if I don't want to get married?* But of course, the questions are spiritual too. How can they not be? As Lesslie Newbigin once wrote: "The story the church is commissioned to tell, if it is true, is bound to call into question any plausibility structure which is founded on other assumptions."[19]

Doubt is not the enemy. It is inevitable. And it is important to understand that humans cannot live in the state of doubt forever. They find a way to resolve the doubt and either strengthen the core belief or reject it for another one. They naturally seek sources to help them process and resolve doubts. They turn first to sources that are seen as safe and knowledgeable in the area. With this in mind, as Christian parents, we want our children coming to us with questions and doubts; we want the doubts brought to the household, not hidden from it; we want to be the safe person who can guide them through this "state of mental disequilibrium."

This does not mean we need to have all the answers—but it does mean that we need to create households where people feel safe to talk about and explore their doubts with the help of loved ones. This is not something to wait for. It is best begun when children are young and naturally bring questions to their parents. These questions can be welcomed and encouraged even as answers are sought together. This

"We need to create households where people feel safe to talk about and explore their doubts with the help of loved ones."

creates a pattern of safety and exploration that will become the norm when children are older. Households should embrace doubt as the way to strengthen and create vibrant faith together.

Shared Activities & Rituals

In many Christian circles today, you'll hear people talk about "doing life" with others. What does that phrase entail, especially when it comes to the individuals we are most likely to "do life" with: our housemates?

In a practical sense, time use surveys give us somewhat of a glimpse. For example, the Bureau of Labor Statistics reports that, on a daily basis, the average American adult with a full-time job will spend about nine of their 24 hours on sleep. After a night's rest, work (6.45) and various forms of leisure (5.24) each take up several hours.[20] Beyond that, there are precious few hours left to divvy up for meals, household duties, caretaking and so on.

Of course, this list from the Bureau of Labor Statistics doesn't account for prayer, Bible-reading, contemplation or other spiritual disciplines. It also can't speak to some of the intangible ways people might view or invest their hours—not as measurements of time, but as opportunities to enjoy someone's company, to learn something new, to impart wisdom, to confront or maybe even to reconcile. One study by health insurer Cigna suggests these more relational tasks aren't well prioritized; half of Americans say they have meaningful daily social interactions, like a heart-to-heart with a friend or quality time with family.[21]

This chapter will focus on the ways in which practicing Christians are truly present and interactive in their homes, shaping not only their everyday rituals but their household roles and spiritual growth.

Regular At-Home Routines Shared with All Household Members

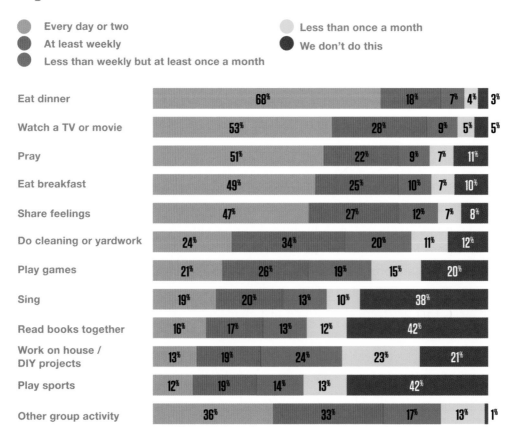

- Every day or two
- At least weekly
- Less than weekly but at least once a month
- Less than once a month
- We don't do this

	Every day or two	At least weekly	Less than weekly but at least once a month	Less than once a month	We don't do this
Eat dinner	68%	18%	7%	4%	3%
Watch a TV or movie	53%	28%	9%	5%	5%
Pray	51%	22%	9%	7%	11%
Eat breakfast	49%	25%	10%	7%	10%
Share feelings	47%	27%	12%	7%	8%
Do cleaning or yardwork	24%	34%	20%	11%	12%
Play games	21%	26%	19%	15%	20%
Sing	19%	20%	13%	10%	38%
Read books together	16%	17%	13%	12%	42%
Work on house / DIY projects	13%	19%	24%	23%	21%
Play sports	12%	19%	14%	13%	42%
Other group activity	36%	33%	17%	13%	1%

n=2,347 U.S. practicing Christian adults and teens, April 5–11, 2018. Question specified these as activities shared with "the people who live with you."

Regular Activities

Typically, if household members are all together, they are gathered around the table (though, as the *Wall Street Journal* reports, some research suggests mealtimes could stand to be a little longer).[22] According to this Barna study, dinner, every day or every other day, is the most common group activity (68%) in Christian households. Half (49%) also include shared breakfast in their routines.

Fifty-three percent of respondents say their housemates regularly come together to watch TV. But they still connect beyond screen time: Nearly half (47%) have discussions about how they are feeling every day or two. Work (such as house projects and yardwork) and play (such as games) are less consistent group activities. Meanwhile, reading books, playing sports and singing are activities that respondents say they never share in their homes (42%, 42% and 38%, respectively).

The data show many household categories strive for some kind of structure or formality. Forty-four percent of respondents mention holding household or family meetings. This occurs most when there are minor residents (59%), especially in nuclear families and multi-generational and single-parent households. Further, a quarter of households (26%) has an agreement about behavior in their homes, such as a roommate contract—which, by the way, a third of roommate households (34%) uses. Such an agreement is uncommon among couples (7%), perhaps because communication is more direct between the two spouses and there are fewer variables than in, say, a multi-generational (40%) or single-parent (38%) context.

Beyond the home, food is also the impetus for togetherness. Three-quarters of respondents (76%), and couples in particular (90%), go out to eat at least once a month as a group. Roommates are least likely to take a trip to a restaurant together (61%).

Spiritual Activities

There is another activity that housemates prioritize venturing out for: worship services. Keep in mind, respondents in this study are all practicing Christians, a categorization that requires them to attend church at least once a month. But respondents report that members of their household, usually their spouses (39%) or kids (31%), attend church on a weekly basis as well. Accordingly, the household types most likely to attend church together are nuclear families (94%) and couples (84%).

What about other forms of faith engagement on their own time at home? The majority of respondents (85%) participates in personal

Household Types & Faith Engagement at Home

% of respondents in each household type who say they do these activities together with their housemates

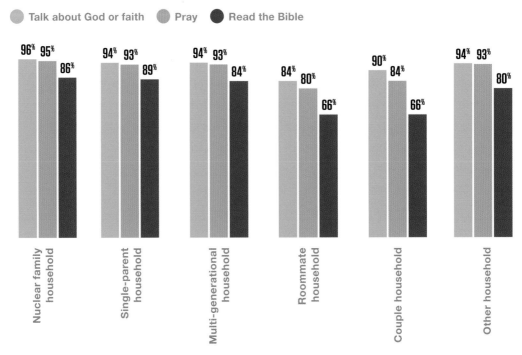

● Talk about God or faith   ● Pray   ● Read the Bible

Nuclear family household: 96% Talk about God or faith, 95% Pray, 86% Read the Bible

Single-parent household: 94% Talk about God or faith, 93% Pray, 89% Read the Bible

Multi-generational household: 94% Talk about God or faith, 93% Pray, 84% Read the Bible

Roommate household: 84% Talk about God or faith, 80% Pray, 66% Read the Bible

Couple household: 90% Talk about God or faith, 84% Pray, 66% Read the Bible

Other household: 94% Talk about God or faith, 93% Pray, 80% Read the Bible

n=2,347 U.S. practicing Christian adults and teens, April 5–11, 2018. Question specified these as activities shared with "the people who live with you."

prayer, and two in five (40%) attend a small group. Most also have spiritual interactions with their housemates, such as talking about God or faith (92%), group prayer (89%) or reading the Bible (78%). Four in 10 respondents (39%) say spiritual conversations occur every day or two.

The data can't truly assess the depth or quality of these actions, and given that even a majority of nominal Christians says talking about God or faith (89%), group prayer (88%) and reading the Bible (74%) are the norm, it's good to remember that faith being commonplace isn't a guarantee that it will be robust. However, these spiritual practices could also be regarded as outcomes on their own—that is, as signs that a household is actively nurturing Christianity. What's more, feeling a sense of responsibility for sharing faith with non-believers correlates with having more spiritual conversations at home—nearly three in four (73%) who hold this belief talk about God or faith weekly in their household—so we can assume these interactions are neither isolated nor absent-minded. Many of these respondents would likely qualify as what the *Spiritual Conversations in the Digital Age* study defined as Eager Conversationalists (Christians who have had 10 or more conversations about faith in the past year), more than three-quarters of whom (77%) feel a responsibility to evangelize.[23]

As noted before, hospitality is also correlated with spiritual habits in the home. Households that have regular visitors other than relatives show a slight but statistically significant lead in their engagement in Bible-reading (86% vs. 73% of those who don't receive regular visitors) or prayer together (93% vs. 87%) or to discuss God and faith (94% vs. 90%). This is understandable given that household activities of any kind are somewhat more common in homes that frequently welcome non-family guests. Sociable atmospheres could be more open to both individuals and interactions, including those related to faith formation, or it's possible that having external influences beyond one's family spurs shared interests and habits even after the guests have gone.

Feeling a sense of responsibility for sharing faith correlates with having more spiritual conversations at home

Shared Activities & Openness to Non-Family Guests

% of respondents in each household type who say they do these activities together with their housemates

● Households that regularly have non-family guests

● Households that don't regularly have non-family guests

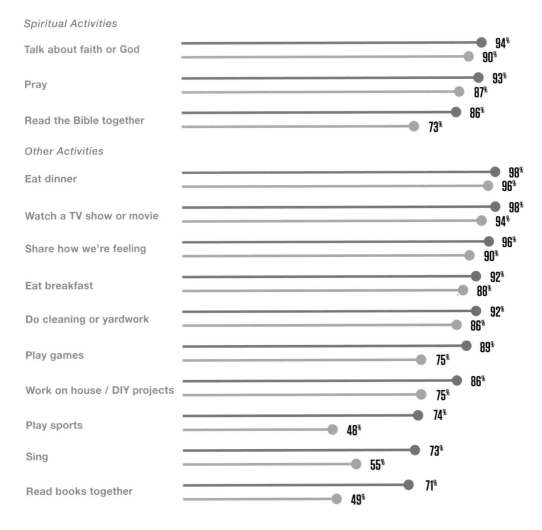

Spiritual Activities

Talk about faith or God
94%
90%

Pray
93%
87%

Read the Bible together
86%
73%

Other Activities

Eat dinner
98%
96%

Watch a TV show or movie
98%
94%

Share how we're feeling
96%
90%

Eat breakfast
92%
88%

Do cleaning or yardwork
92%
86%

Play games
89%
75%

Work on house / DIY projects
86%
75%

Play sports
74%
48%

Sing
73%
55%

Read books together
71%
49%

n=2,347 U.S. practicing Christian adults and teens, April 5–11, 2018. Question specified these as activities shared with "the people who live with you."

Kids Are a Catalyst for **Any** Household Activity

Houses with kids around are typically bigger and busier, and likely require adults to involve or instruct children in a range of tasks. So it's probably not a surprise that most regular routines or rituals, whether recreational, practical or spiritual, are more common when minors are present. Even activities rarely done as a group, like chores, sports, taking walks or going to the park, increase when children are present.

Similarly, statistical modeling shows that—more than relationship status, age, household type or any other influential factor—the presence of minors is a major driver of spiritual interactions in a home, such as group Bible-reading (87% vs. 68% of homes without minors), prayer (95% vs. 83%) or conversations about God and faith (95% vs. 88%).

Naturally, kids provide opportunities for housemates to spend more time together, often thoughtfully so, whether cooking a meal,

> The presence
> of minors is a
> major driver
> of spiritual
> interactions
> in a home

Activities Outside the Home and the Effect of Minors

% of respondents in each household type who say they do these activities together with their housemates

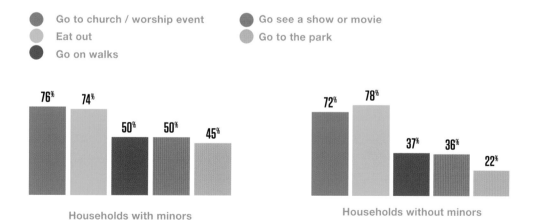

- ● Go to church / worship event
- ○ Eat out
- ● Go on walks
- ● Go see a show or movie
- ○ Go to the park

Households with minors: 76% · 74% · 50% · 50% · 45%

Households without minors: 72% · 78% · 37% · 36% · 22%

n=2,347 U.S. practicing Christian adults and teens. April 5–11, 2018. Question specified these as activities shared with "the people who live with you."

Spiritual Activities and the Effect of Minors

% of respondents in each household type who say they do these activities together with their housemates

● Talk about God or faith　　● Pray　　● Read the Bible

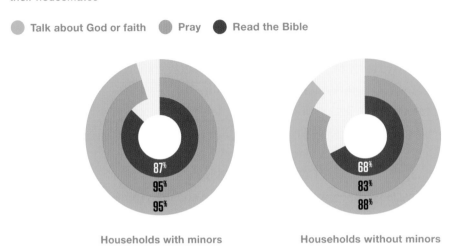

Households with minors	Households without minors

n=2,347 U.S. practicing Christian adults and teens, April 5–11, 2018. Question specified these as activities shared with "the people who live with you."

completing homework, participating in athletics or, yes, growing in faith. Spiritually, to a certain extent, we're observing some families in the process of modeling or "passing down" faith to their children. As the previous chapter explains (page 40), that alone does not lead to rich, lifelong belief, and extended housemates and outside influences appear to be crucial players in spiritual formation as well. But kids don't just require much of us; they quite literally ask much. Their curiosity and impressionability in all things, including faith, could incite earnest spiritual discussions and disciplines in the Christian adults in their vicinity as well. These are teachable moments for both adult and child that could do them a lot of spiritual good.

For couple households, roommate households or other environments without children present, it's possible that spiritual development is less of a shared, in-house endeavor—or perhaps even stalls.

Of course, this data set alone can't speak to the nature or strength of spiritual interactions beyond one's household. But it does pose questions for faith leaders: As you consider the long-term spiritual formation of young people, how do you also encourage today's adults toward a strong faith in every season of life? What is there to learn from the presence or mindset of children that can be replicated in any household context? And what is each church member's duty in shaping the faith of the next generation, regardless of when or whether young people are in their direct care?

Generally Active Households Are Spiritually Active Households

If we're regarding any effort toward faith formation in the household as an outcome on its own, and if we're seeking to understand what distinguishes the people who prioritize these efforts, it's instructive to know that they are the same people who appear to make any activity a priority. Welcoming guests, watching TV, sharing breakfast and other routines and rituals are also common in households that carve out time to read the Bible, pray or talk about God together. Conversely, households that do not engage in faith-based group activities are much more likely not to do anything together (31% of those who do not have spiritual conversations, 23% of those who do not pray or read the Bible together).

In short, practicing Christians who intentionally cultivate a spiritual environment in their household are simply intentional to begin with. Barna has seen a similar correlation in some of its other reports, where positive tendencies are not exclusive, but hang together: In a study of perceptions of global poverty, the more someone cared about one issue, the more they cared about any injustice;[24] in a study of vocation, the more someone was attuned to faith, the more they were

Practicing Christians who intentionally cultivate a spiritual environment in their household are simply intentional to begin with

All Household Activities, by Participation in Shared Prayer, Bible-Reading or Spiritual Conversations

% of respondents in each household faith engagement category who say they do these activities together with their housemates

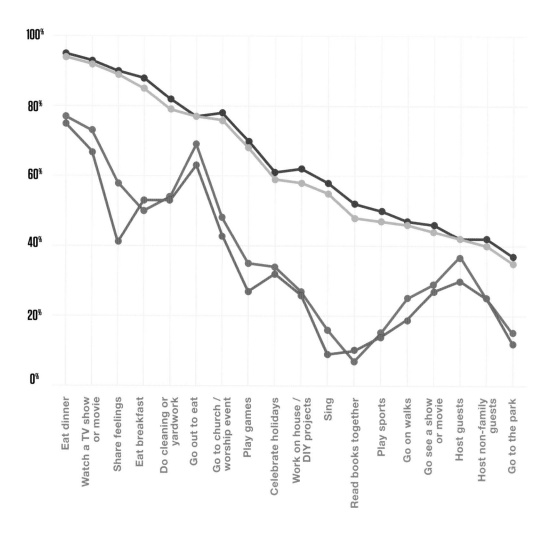

● Spiritual conversations   ● No spiritual conversations

● Shared prayer or Bible-reading   ● No shared prayer or Bible-reading

n≈2,347 U.S. practicing Christian adults and teens, April 5–11, 2018. Question specified these as activities shared at least monthly with "the people who live with you."

attuned to their work.[25] Similarly, in this study of Christian households, the more housemates engage in general activity, the more they engage in spiritual activity.

One-on-One Interactions in Households

Group activities aren't the only engagement that defines a practicing Christian household. Particularly when there are more residents, it's safe to assume dynamics in individual relationships contribute to the overall mood, routines and spiritual climate of the home. In this respect, roommate households are the least interactive. But many members of households and extended households engage with one another in a number of dimensions, a diversity of interactions that can have a positive correlation with the overall atmosphere and spiritual nourishment of a home. Good fun, good work and good faith seem to go hand in hand, indicating spiritual growth is yet another way of being present, interested and engaged in the lives of those around you, or vice versa.

As mentioned in chapter two, the TV screen acts as a hearth for house-wide gatherings, and this also tends to be true of one-on-one interactions; in most household relationships, watching a movie or show is a main activity in any dynamic.

Regular one-on-one interactions occur most between spouses. Respondents speaking of their husband or wife describe the daily activities of a partnership, both mundane and meaningful: keeping in touch, eating meals, confronting one another, watching TV, praying together and, importantly, having fun .

The data also show that relationships between husbands and wives could be complicated when kids enter the picture. Even though couples generally tend to orbit each other at home, that connection isn't quite as prominent in households with minors present. If kids are in the home, adult practicing Christians' responses show the

Continued on page 68.

How Households Feel

Practicing Christians Describe the Atmospheres of Their Homes

One of the major aims of this project was to evaluate the perceived emotional climate of Christians' households. Roughly two-thirds of practicing Christians say the atmosphere of their households are *comfortable* (69%), *loving* (67%) and *safe* (65%), which are the top descriptors overall. Respondents who have spiritual conversations or worship with household members typically say their homes are *loving, safe, peaceful, joyful, nurturing* and other attractive characteristics.

Hospitable homes are more likely than those that don't regularly welcome guests to be *nurturing* and *joyful*, as well as *intellectual* and *artistic*, perhaps a sign of being stimulated by frequent guests.

Some of the adjectives one might assume are generally positive don't always pop up in environments that carry other key markers of a healthy, faith-centered household, such as hospitality or spiritual conversations. For instance, couple households have an array of good feelings about their home atmosphere, and this category's predominant age group, the Boomers, are mostly *comfortable*—but we also see that these are less interactive households with more limited communities. In this case, perhaps, *comfortable*

has also led to some complacency in the bounds of familiarity.

Meanwhile, households with minors, in which respondents also claim a variety of close outside relationships, tend to be *joyful, messy, playful, nurturing* and even *old-fashioned*, but less likely to be *peaceful, casual* and *comfortable*.

Barna's *Spiritual Conversations in the Digital Age* report offers some interesting emotional parallels: Christians who have had at least 10 conversations about faith in the past year often associate these spiritual discussions with peace and joy, or even report that laughter was a part of their last spiritual conversation (70%).[26]

Comfort and safety are nice, but not always conduits for growth, which often requires a certain stretching outside one's comfort zone. Developing authentic faith and sharing it with others appears to be a little looser, messier and more human.

Feels Like Home

The routines, activities and relationships of a household all work together to create an atmosphere, a certain character or undercurrent that defines the home. When asked to describe their households, most Christians use positive—indeed, homey—language.

Comfortable: 69% / Loving: 67% / Safe: 65% / Peaceful: 55% / Casual: 54% / Joyful: 51% / Playful: 41% / Nurturing: 38% / Old-fashioned: 25% / Intellectual: 22% / Artistic: 14% / Messy: 14% / Tense: 9% / Crowded: 6% / Secretive: 6% / Sad: 4% / In crisis: 3%

n=2,347 U.S. practicing Christian adult and teens, April 5-11, 2018.

Atmosphere in Different Types of Households

% of respondents in each household type who use this adjective to describe their household atmosphere

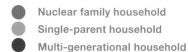

- Nuclear family household
- Single-parent household
- Multi-generational household
- Roommate household
- Couple household

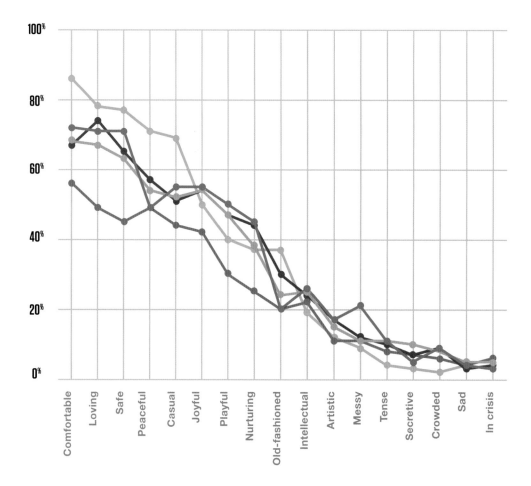

n=2,347 U.S. practicing Christian adults and teens, April 5–11, 2018.

Types of One-on-One Interactions Across Household Types

% of respondents in each household type who say they have done this activity with any member of their household or extended household in the past month

Nuclear family household
Single-parent household
Roommate household
Multi-generational household
Couple household
Other

We eat meals together
92%
89%
76%
93%
96%
89%

We watch TV or movies together
90%
85%
68%
87%
92%
84%

We have fun together
91%
86%
66%
88%
89%
85%

We talk about God and faith
84%
82%
64%
86%
78%
77%

We work around the house together
82%
73%
59%
79%
81%
73%

We pray together
76%
73%
55%
79%
71%
70%

We confront each other
76%
70%
55%
75%
75%
66%

We play sports together
58%
44%
34%
47%
14%
39%

n~2,347 U.S. practicing Christian adults and teens, April 5–11, 2018. Respondents were only shown relationship types they live with or who visit them regularly in their home.

relationship between spouses becomes less dominant. Interactions between children and their parents—primarily mothers—become the heart of household routines and activities (explored more on page 105). Given that older couple households in this sample are less socially connected, spouses may begin to lean on and enjoy each other's company in a new way once they have finished their child-rearing years.

For those who have never married, including teenage respondents, most one-on-one household interactions are less frequent, but primarily occur with mothers and siblings. Those who are no longer married (widowed, divorced or separated) intersect most with their children. Across the board, children become the go-to housemates for having fun or playing sports, categories in which siblings also jump in the ranks.

Connecting via Technology

Even in this digital era, in-person activities are still at the core of practicing Christians' individual relationships and interactions with housemates. However, respondents do sometimes connect with household members—usually their spouses or children—through devices.

Of a few forms of tech-based communication, social media is the one household members rarely use to keep in touch, probably because they are regularly in the same space. People tend to have more contact with Mom than Dad in their texting, calling or commenting. Respondents freely text and email their friends and siblings, but less often actually place a call to them.

Just because devices aren't the primary tool for nurturing in-household connections doesn't mean devices aren't restructuring our home lives. According to Barna research conducted for Andy Crouch's book *The Tech-Wise Family*, a lot of parents feel it's harder

Primary Connections in Households Without Minors

% say they have done this activity with this member of their household or extended household in the past month

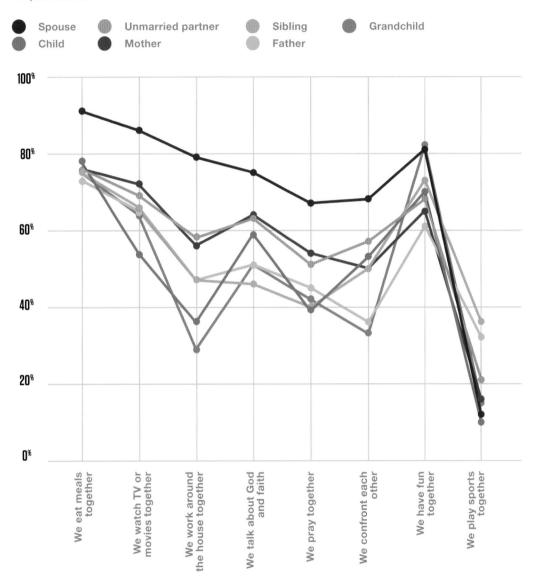

● Spouse   ● Unmarried partner   ● Sibling   ● Grandchild

● Child   ● Mother   ● Father

n=1,032 U.S. practicing Christian adults and teens without kids <18 at home, April 5–11, 2018. Respondents were only shown relationship types they live with or who visit them regularly in their home. Most of these categories are only 100-200 people, with a sample error of 8–10 percent.

Primary Connections in Households with Minors

% say they have done this activity with this member of their household or extended household in the past month

● Child   ● Friend   ● Mother   ● Father
● Spouse ● Sibling ● Roommate

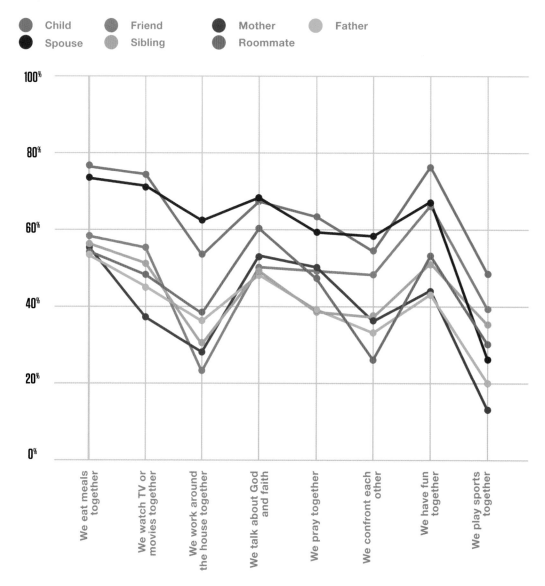

n=1,315 U.S. practicing Christian adults and teens with minors in the home, April 5–11, 2018. Respondents were only shown relationship types they live with or who visit them regularly in their home. Most of these categories are only 100–200 people, with a sample error of 8–10 percent. Categories removed due to small sample include: grandparent, stepchild, grandchild, unmarried partner.

than ever to raise kids, and in their view, the main culprit is technology and social media (64%).[27] On the other end of the equation, most adults say they never take time away from social media. So while this study analyzes the many in-person interactions that housemates and families share, we should assume that people are often accompanied by glowing screens and perhaps digitally interacting with those outside the household at the same time.

Communication Among Various Household Members

% of respondents in each household type who say they do these activities together with their housemates or extended household in the past month

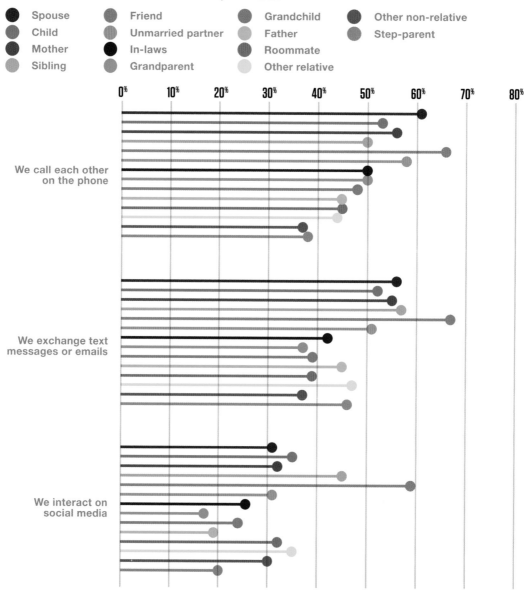

● Spouse
● Child
● Mother
● Sibling
● Friend
● Unmarried partner
● In-laws
● Grandparent
● Grandchild
● Father
● Roommate
● Other relative
● Other non-relative
● Step-parent

We call each other on the phone

We exchange text messages or emails

We interact on social media

n=2,347 U.S. practicing Christian adults and teens, April 5–11, 2018. Respondents were only shown relationship types they live with or who visit them regularly in their home.

Growing Up but Not Moving Out

A Peek at the Modern Rise of All-Adult Nuclear Families

As of 2015, U.S. Census Bureau data reported that a third of young adults ages 18 to 34 lived with their parents.[28] Even a year later, nearly all of this group (88%) continued to crash with Mom and Dad. Many of these Millennials went to college only to boomerang back to live in their parents' homes. A number of economic factors may contribute to this and other distinctives of Millennials' early adulthood experience: increased housing costs, lower post-recession wages, high student loan debt and more.

The surge in this type of all-adult or "grown-up" nuclear family has been dramatic, so much so that the U.S. Census Bureau recently identified it as the most popular living arrangement for young adults in the U.S. In the decade between 2005 and 2015, the proportion of young adults living with their parents increased from 26 percent to 34 percent. Commentators may lament "freeloading" Millennials and their extended adolescence, and indeed, among Americans between ages 25 and 34 who lived with their parents in 2016, a quarter was not actively working or in school. But overall, independent living of any kind has become less common among young adults, dropping 10 percentage points during that same period.[29] The motivations for either moving in with peers or moving back in with parents appear to be a mix of both cost-cutting and cultural shifts. *The Atlantic* notes in one article about roommate relationships that even "a recovering economy hasn't led young people to change course."[30]

In this research study of practicing Christians, Barna singled out nuclear family households made up entirely of adults—as in single

Major Differences Between Grown-up Nuclear Families and the Average Household

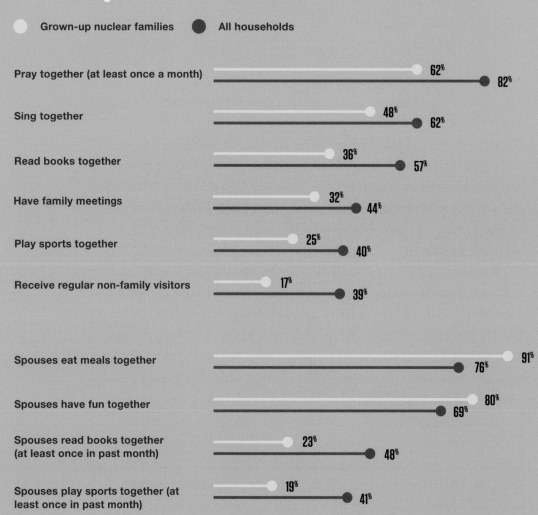

● Grown-up nuclear families   ● All households

Pray together (at least once a month)
62%
82%

Sing together
48%
62%

Read books together
36%
57%

Have family meetings
32%
44%

Play sports together
25%
40%

Receive regular non-family visitors
17%
39%

Spouses eat meals together
91%
76%

Spouses have fun together
80%
69%

Spouses read books together (at least once in past month)
23%
48%

Spouses play sports together (at least once in past month)
19%
41%

n=2,347 U.S. practicing Christian adults and teens, April 5–11, 2018. Respondents were only shown relationship types they live with or who visit them regularly in their home.

adult children (usually Millennials) living with both of their parents (usually Boomers)—for closer examination. They make up a small proportion (5%) of the total sample, as young practicing Christians who don't live alone appear to favor roommate households. We find that the behaviors of this family unit differ from the average household and the traditional nuclear family category in some notable ways.

The biggest difference may be that **grown-up nuclear families aren't quite as interactive and fun.** They are less likely than nuclear families with kids to play sports, read books or sing together. Gathering, in general, is less common, whether for hosting guests or having household meetings. Further, mothers with adult children at home also seem to step back from some of the spiritual coaching that is typical when minors are in the household—perhaps one reason why nuclear households with young children are more likely to come together to attend church or pray.

The nature of the parents' marriage also shifts when only adult children live with them. It's reasonable to assume these spouses, similar to those in couple households, spend more time together; Barna sees this is especially true of mealtimes. But these interactions, though consistent—and, as 80 percent of married respondents in grown-up nuclear families tell Barna, even fun—may not be as purposeful as when parents are in a season of raising children. For instance, when looking at the grown-up nuclear context, we see a dip in spouses participating in everything from encouraging one another to working on house projects together.

In short, the all-adult nuclear family is less engaged than the bustling standard nuclear family. In some ways, they take on the qualities of a roommate household (or of a couple household with a beloved extended household member). Naturally, adult offspring have a level of independence that minor children don't have, cultivating more of their own life, career and community outside of the home and requiring

Major Differences Between Nuclear Families with and Without Minors

● Grown-up nuclear families ● Nuclear families (with minors)

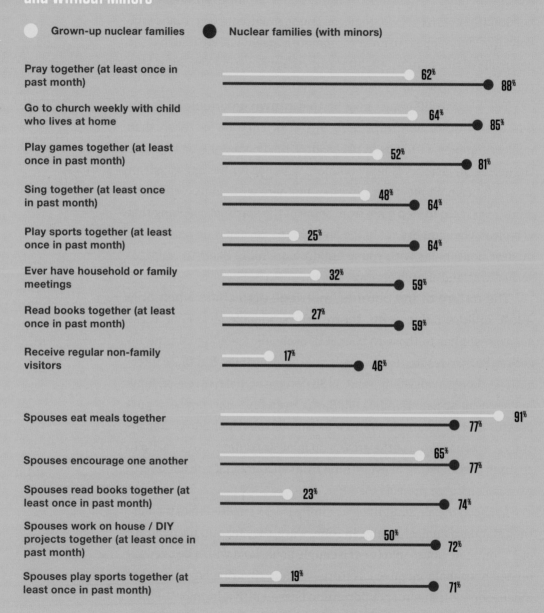

Pray together (at least once in past month)
62%
88%

Go to church weekly with child who lives at home
64%
85%

Play games together (at least once in past month)
52%
81%

Sing together (at least once in past month)
48%
64%

Play sports together (at least once in past month)
25%
64%

Ever have household or family meetings
32%
59%

Read books together (at least once in past month)
27%
59%

Receive regular non-family visitors
17%
46%

Spouses eat meals together
77%
91%

Spouses encourage one another
65%
77%

Spouses read books together (at least once in past month)
23%
74%

Spouses work on house / DIY projects together (at least once in past month)
50%
72%

Spouses play sports together (at least once in past month)
19%
71%

n=795 U.S. practicing Christian adults and teens who live in nuclear family households or grown-up nuclear family households, April 5–11, 2018. Respondents were only shown relationship types they live with or who visit them regularly in their home.

less involvement from their parents. It's also possible that, because this living arrangement carries a certain amount of stigma in modern Western contexts, its occupants are prone to treat it as impermanent. With no clear roles, the responsibilities and activities that ordinarily strengthen the bonds and faith of housemates seem to fall by the wayside.

What do we make of this familial but not familiar context? It depends on who you ask. In 2018 alone, two different studies in the UK offered conflicting conclusions about the effects of boomerang kids, one showing a decline in parents' well-being, the other showing improved relationships.[31] Further, popular understanding of what is "normal" or healthy for families is always shifting and depends greatly on the resources and motivations of a particular society and time. After all, the concept of the American nuclear family now regarded as "traditional" is a fairly recent invention of the 1950s, and multi-generational family households play a more central role in other regions.[32] It remains to be seen how long U.S. adults will find this grown-up nuclear family an appealing option, but in the meantime, practicing Christians within these households have an opportunity to set a precedent. If the findings of this Barna study are any guide, some universal recommendations apply: Spend intentional, enjoyable time together, and open your doors to others.

Connecting Old & Young in the Family of God

A Q&A with David Meggers

More than any other category, couple households (primarily Boomers and Elders) have a solitary lifestyle where spouses somewhat orbit each other. What factors do you think might contribute to that? What might these couples gain or lose in these years when they are so reliant on one another?

We know Boomers are living longer and experiencing better health and mobility. Yet many are choosing early retirement, and often there is not a plan for post-retirement. Cut loose from the work community, the Boomer has lost a long-cultivated community, which is perhaps now reduced to only their spouse—who may or may not be ready for this much spousal time. Since Boomers are less likely to be "joiners," there is a relationship void. These tendencies lead me to believe that more of the "orbit" is due to their pre-retirement choices rather than their circumstances.

There may be an opportunity to gain a greater appreciation for community. There might also be a willingness to forego the solitary life and seek to engage in church, organizations and volunteer efforts. Churches have long been strong organizationally, but not always relationally. Churches that elevate the relational aspects of the Christian faith may stand a good chance of gaining an audience with the Boomer.

David Meggers

Associate pastor at Concordia Lutheran Church

David is the unit executive for adult and older adult ministries at Concordia Lutheran Church in Kirkwood, Missouri. Previously, he has been a teacher, athletic coach and church planter, and he spent 24 years serving and pastoring at Christ the Rock Lutheran Church in Southeast Rockford, Illinois. He holds a BS in Education from Concordia University St. Paul and an MDiv and STM from Concordia Seminary, St. Louis.

What is the power of cross-generational relationships or multi-generational households when it comes to spiritual growth? Do you see older Christians and grandparents growing aware of a role in leaving a faith legacy?

Part of the power in the grandparent relationship comes from the space afforded by the generational distance. Mom or Dad typically have to deal with the almost constant pressures, needs and expectations of parenting, giving them little space for the kinds of conversations and experiences grandparents can offer. Grandparents have garnered wisdom—another way of saying they have learned from their own mistakes and successes as parents. They have the margin to act rather than react. Their interactions are less emotionally laden. The grandkids can sense their more laidback attitude compared to their parents, who are the primary disciplinarians.

I think older Christians do exhibit a growing awareness of having a role in leaving a faith legacy. This observation is borne out by conversations in which these adults lament their perceived failure in passing on the faith to their own children and now see the opportunity and necessity of leaving a faith legacy with their grandchildren. Older

Christians are also aware of the increased societal pressures on the family and the resultant challenges to faith life in families. They recognize that they can be a helping hand in the faith formation of their grandchildren and, to some extent, have a second chance to influence the faith development of their adult children. This helping hand will best be received if it is not heavy, but rather a gentle, loving, receiving, giving and kind hand. I also see this faith legacy awareness exhibit itself in the volunteerism of older adults regarding the educational ministries of our church.

Beyond our own families or households, what is our responsibility to one another, old and young, as church members? How can ministries speak to this and foster opportunities to connect different age groups and allow them to learn from each other?

"We can be more responsible to one another by appreciating one another as fellow baptized children of God, rather than being so delineated by our age categories."

The Church is the body of Christ. All the parts of the body are different. Not only do its members have different gifts, they are experiencing different seasons of life. The church has a responsibility to speak to this holistic reality. We can be more responsible to one another by appreciating one another as fellow baptized children of God, rather than being so delineated by our age categories. Younger generations can learn to appreciate older generations for their wisdom and experience, if that wisdom and experience is not lorded over the younger generations. Older generations can be more accepting and encouraging to younger generations by giving them the space they need to grow in their faith and respecting their articulation of that faith.

Special Sundays could emphasize the intergenerational nature of the church. The disparaging attitudes and remarks of ageism and youthism need to be called out as offensive to one another and to God. Perhaps a greater emphasis on "honoring father and mother" and "parents not provoking children" need to be examined through the lens of intergenerational ministry. Rather than compartmentalizing ministries by the metric of age, other metrics such as interests, personality types, even geography (neighborhoods) might be good avenues to allow the generations to work with each other, experience one another and learn from each other.

What would your advice be for parents of grown children who, often because of economic circumstances, are sharing their space again? How can they stay present and establish healthy and spiritual routines with one another, even if they regard this as a temporary arrangement?

Boundaries would seem to be a huge topic of conversation. When the children are younger, there are curfews, house rules, perhaps even chores. Parental expectations will need to be examined in these areas. Is the parent still to be the provider of food and shelter? Or will there be an expectation (stated and agreed upon) that the young adult will be a contributor to housing expenses, food expenses or duties around the house? In addition, the conversation needs to include how to treat one another's guests, or the expectations of guests in general. Key to all of this is the cultivation of conversation, and this needs to begin very early in life so that young adult and parent can more meaningfully have these often emotion-laden conversations with more thoughtfulness. Hopefully these households will capitalize on the earlier cultivation of faith in the family in such a way that they grow with one another in their faith. Parent-child retreats and Bible studies might be good to develop. In addition, the opportunities for families to serve together should produce fruit.

Relationships to Rely On

4

In a 2011 study comparing Americans' circle of acquaintances with their inner circle or "trust network," the latter proved to be much smaller—and shrinking. "The mean size of core networks ... dropped from 2.9 out of a maximum of five in 1985 to 2.1 in 2004, with 22.5% of the sample listing no names at all," the report from University of Wisconsin—Madison and Columbia University details.[33] Cigna's "loneliness index" also finds that roughly one-fifth of Americans rarely or never feels close to people or that there is someone they can talk to.[34] Similarly, in a 2015 Barna survey, nearly one-third of Americans (31%) admits they have no one in their local area—outside of family members—who they could rely on for help and support in the event of an emergency or tough situation. These bleak findings about the general population point to a deficit of intimacy and community. Do those in the Church fare any better, if only in their own homes?

Barna wanted to identify not only the housemates with whom practicing Christians most interact, but the housemates they trust—the confidants and most reliable members within one's household or extended household.

As you'll see in the following pages, there are a number of close relationships, family and otherwise, that shape and uplift practicing Christians. But some clear patterns emerge early and often, and they tend to be an extension of the relationships that benefit from the most one-on-one interactions. In other words, our most frequent

Who Are You Most Likely to Go to for...?

	Advice	Money	Sympathy	Logistical help	Encouragement
1	Spouse 80%	Spouse 81%	Spouse 66%	Spouse 63%	Spouse 72%
2	Unmarried partner 73%	Father 61%	Unmarried partner 63%	Father 50%	Mother 62%
3	Mother 66%	Unmarried partner 59%	Mother 58%	Unmarried partner 49%	Grandparent 62%
4	Friend 63%	Mother 56%	Grandparent 53%	Mother 48%	Unmarried partner 59%
5	Grandparent 53%	Grandparent 49%	Friend 52%	Friend 40%	Father 49%
6	Father 50%	Step-parent 46%	Sibling 42%	Roommate 40%	Sibling 49%
7	Roommate 49%	Roommate 40%	Roommate 38%	Grandparent 38%	Roommate 45%
8	Sibling 49%	Sibling 28%	Child 36%	Step-parent 36%	Child 43%
9	Other relative 32%	Friend 24%	Father 34%	Sibling 34%	Friend 40%
10	Step-parent 31%	Other relative 22%	Step-parent 30%	Other non-relative 34%	Other relative 36%
11	In-laws 29%	Child 21%	Other relative 26%	Child 32%	Step-parent 34%
12	Other non-relative 29%	In-laws 16%	Other non-relative 26%	In-laws 28%	In-laws 33%
13	Child 28%	Other non-relative 16%	In-laws 21%	Other relative 22%	Other non-relative 29%
14	Grandchild 12%	Grandchild 7%	Grandchild 15%	Grandchild 13%	Grandchild 24%

n=2,347 U.S. practicing Christian adults and teens, April 5–11, 2018. Respondents were only shown relationship types they live with or who visit them regularly in their home.

companions and our most dependable ones tend to be the same. Thus, time and again, responses suggest that the women who raise us or the people we marry have the greatest potential for impact.

Our most frequent companions and our most dependable ones tend to be the same

Lean on Me: Where Housemates Get Help

Practical & Emotional Support

Depending on their season of life or relationship status, practicing Christians point to two core relationships they depend on most: a spouse or a parent (usually their mother). The previous chart illustrates how well-rounded these relationships are in providing practical assistance or an emotional boost.

Overall, married people mainly go to their spouses for money (81%), advice (80%), encouragement (72%), sympathy (66%) or logistical help (63%). Second to their spouse, they rely next on their own children (likely grown) to address these needs. They are less likely than unmarried adults to depend on close friends, siblings or their own parents. Yet just as the presence of minors affects respondents' regular interactions with spouses, households begin to pull from a wider circle for help, advice or companionship when kids are around. This seems organic, since the number of frequent guests increases in households with children, and parents might require a variety of input in best caring for kids.

Essentially, the addition of children to a household may result in a couple shifting their reliance on each other to others in their household network—and, depending on the couple, that could be good or bad for a marriage. Are mothers who take on the bulk of parenting duties (which, as explored on page 105, is common) left with little to give to their connection with their spouse? Could the priority placed on relationships with children contribute to fathers' general detachment

Top Sources of Support for Married Practicing Christian Adults

% of married respondents who say they are most likely to go to this member of their household or extended household for ...

● Spouse ● Friend ● Roommate ● Child
● Mother ● Father ● Sibling

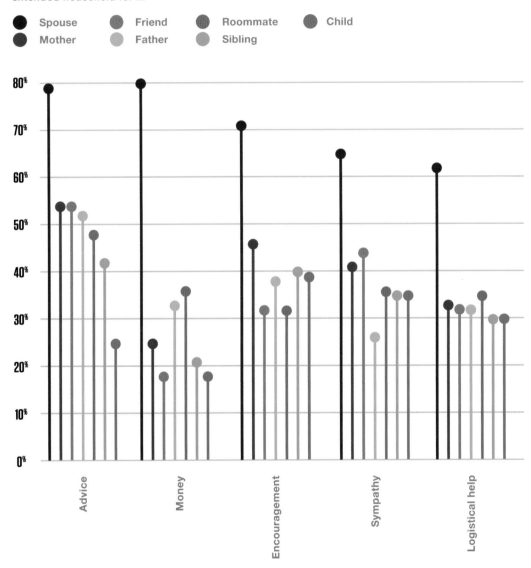

n≈1,275 U.S. married practicing Christian adults, April 5–11, 2018. Respondents were only shown relationship types they live with or who visit them regularly in their homes.

Top Sources of Support for Unmarried Practicing Christian Adults

% of unmarried respondents who say they are most likely to go to this member of their household or extended household for ...

- Unmarried partner
- Mother
- Friend
- Grandparent
- Sibling
- Father
- Roommate

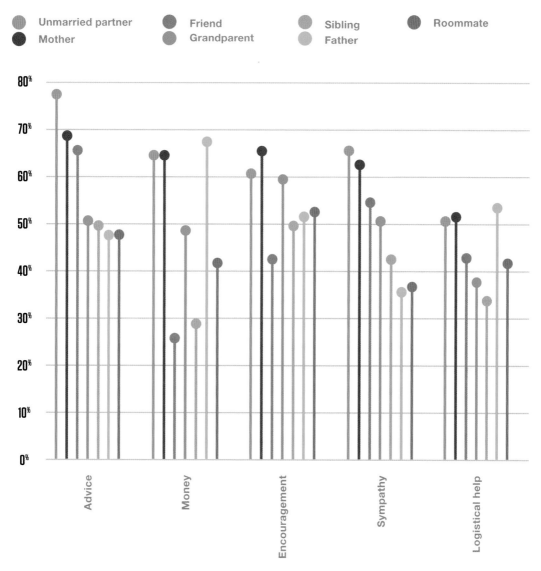

n=624 U.S. unmarried practicing Christian adults, April 5–11, 2018. Respondents were only shown relationship types they live with or who visit them regularly in their homes.

The addition
of children to
a household
causes a couple
to shift their
reliance on each
other to others in
their household
network

or isolation from the rest of the family unit and routines? Or could a broader network of friends, teachers and confidants highlight the unique qualities of a marriage bond, allowing spouses to be partners in the household and family in a way they might not if they were clinging to or existing alongside one another?

Unmarried adults have a more diverse mix of household and extended household members on whom they depend, but mothers still top the list for these single respondents, usually alongside significant others. This is true for advice (70%), encouragement (67%), money (66%) sympathy (64%) or logistical help (53%). Friends also play a big role in meeting single respondents' softer needs (67% advice, 56% sympathy, 44% encouragement and 44% logistical help). After these reliable relationships, fathers, grandparents and housemates follow. For older singles, children are also considered a resource.

Tough Discussions & Big Questions

The theme of dependence on spouses or significant others and mothers continues when looking at discussions about serious issues or faith questions, with some exceptions: For the most part, practicing Christians welcome deep conversations with their mothers, just as long as sex or politics don't come up.

Actually, sex is the issue that, with the exception of romantic partners, all respondents are least likely to discuss with anyone in their households or extended households. Couples have an obvious confidant in this case; overall, spouses (74%) or significant others (68%) are the primary conversation partner when it comes to sex. Married couples with young children are more likely to talk about sex than households without children (72% vs. 65%). If unmarried people are talking about sex with someone other than a significant other, it's usually with a close friend (51%), before siblings (32%), mothers (30%) or housemates (28%). Male and female respondents diverge somewhat

Who Are You Most Likely to Talk with About...?

	Questions about faith	Something that bothers you	Sex	The Bible	Politics
1	Spouse 73%	Spouse 79%	Spouse 74%	Spouse 71%	Spouse 67%
2	Mother 59%	Unmarried partner 68%	Unmarried partner 68%	Unmarried partner 62%	Unmarried partner 55%
3	Unmarried partner 55%	Mother 60%	Friend 39%	Mother 61%	Father 51%
4	Grandparent 55%	Friend 59%	Roommate 26%	Grandparent 60%	Mother 42%
5	Roommate 50%	Sibling 47%	Mother 24%	Father 51%	Roommate 40%
6	Father 49%	Roommate 46%	Father 19%	Friend 45%	Friend 38%
7	Friend 47%	Grandparent 40%	Step-parent 18%	Roommate 45%	Step-parent 37%
8	Step-parent 33%	Father 39%	Sibling 15%	Child 45%	Grandparent 36%
9	Child 32%	Child 38%	Other non-relative 13%	Step-parent 38%	Sibling 30%
10	Sibling 32%	Step-parent 32%	Grandparent 12%	Sibling 36%	Other non-relative 29%
11	Other relative 28%	Other relative 30%	Other relative 12%	Grandchild 35%	In-laws 29%
12	In-laws 25%	Other non-relative 26%	Child 8%	Other relative 32%	Other relative 26%
13	Other non-relative 24%	In-laws 21%	Grandchild 5%	Other non-relative 29%	Child 25%
14	Grandchild 19%	Grandchild 13%	In-laws 2%	In-laws 28%	Grandchild 13%

n=2,347 U.S. practicing Christian adults and teens, April 5-11, 2018. Respondents were only shown relationship types they live with or who visit them regularly in their home.

in whether they would talk to their mother or father about some sensitive matters, especially sex. Looking only at the men and women who indicate having a father and / or mother in the household or extended household, one-third of men (32%) talks to their dads, rather than their moms (8%), about this subject. A similar trend plays out among women and their mothers (29% talk to their mothers, 17% to their fathers).

After spouses, Millennials are most likely to talk to their mothers, friends or roommates about many sensitive topics. More than any other generation, Boomers say they discuss these delicate subjects with no one.

Regardless of the relationship, the Bible is a subject that practicing Christians don't shy away from in their households—but, presumably, those conversations don't delve into scriptural stories and principles that apply to the other difficult topics respondents appear to avoid.

Coping with Crisis

Nearly three in four respondents (73%) say that a member of their household helped them in their last personal crisis. This is most likely in couple households (80%) and least likely in roommate households (66%).

The most helpful bonds in a crisis are—you guessed it—spouses and mothers. Siblings, fathers and, to a lesser extent, children are often involved, though at lower levels. Across generations, most respondents received the most help in their last personal crisis from spouses. For unmarried adults, 45 percent turn to their mothers, followed by fathers, roommates or their own children.

There is some correlation between sharing spiritual interactions in the home and having each other's backs. Three-quarters of those whose households participate in prayer and scripture study (76% vs. 56% of those who do not pray or read the Bible together) or conversations about faith (76% vs. 43% of who do not talk about God and

Establishing rituals of worship together could build an intimacy that enables relationships to be more supportive in times of need

faith together) recall having a housemate who walked alongside them through a crisis. Establishing rituals of worship together could build an intimacy that enables relationships to be more supportive in times of need.

Most Supportive Relationships in Personal Crisis

% of respondents in each household type who say this member of their household helped them in their last personal crisis

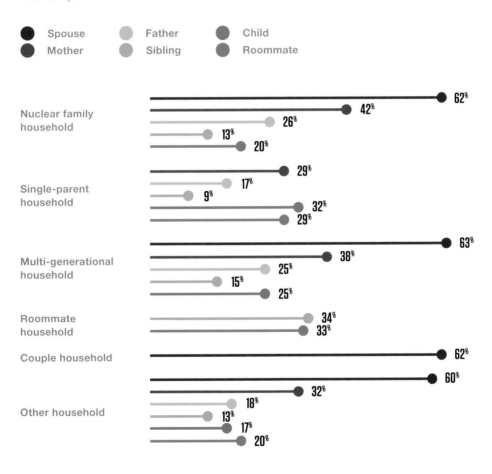

● Spouse   ● Father   ● Child
● Mother   ● Sibling   ● Roommate

Nuclear family household
- 62%
- 42%
- 26%
- 13%
- 20%

Single-parent household
- 29%
- 17%
- 9%
- 32%
- 29%

Multi-generational household
- 63%
- 38%
- 25%
- 15%
- 25%

Roommate household
- 34%
- 33%

Couple household
- 62%

Other household
- 60%
- 32%
- 18%
- 13%
- 17%
- 20%

n=1,725 U.S. practicing Christian adults and teens who say someone they live with helped them through a crisis, April 5–11, 2018. Respondents were only shown relationship types they live with. Missing values mean either this person isn't in the household or that the sample size is too small to show.

Households That Receive Help from Non-Resident Family

Do you depend on family members who do not live in your home to help with finances, childcare or other things to keep your household running? Select all that apply.

- ● Receive help with finances
- ● Receive help with childcare
- ● Receive help with something else that keeps the household running
- ● No, our household rarely or never depends on relatives who don't live here

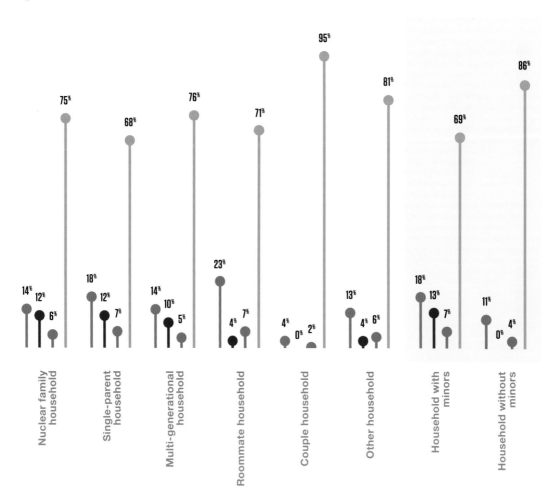

n=1,899 U.S. practicing Christian adults, April 5–11, 2018.

Aid from Other Relatives

A fifth of practicing Christian adult respondents (21%) says their household depends on family members within another household for help. This could apply to finances (14%), but also childcare (6%) or other forms of assistance (5%).

Couple households receive the least help (5%), as they are likely established Boomers, or Millennials with dual income, no dependents and fewer needs. Those in roommate households, who have the lowest average income, tend to receive assistance in the form of financial aid. Thus, we see three in 10 Millennials (29%) report getting some help with money (compared to 12% Gen X, 5% Boomers and 3% Elders).

A third of households with children (31%), especially those led by single parents (32%), receives some kind of help from other relatives. Adults in households with minors usually identify their mothers as a source of help (34%), which could be because moms are stepping into their role as grandparents or remaining on hand for childcare. Comparing help from moms and dads, the most exaggerated differences appear in nuclear families (36% mothers vs. 11% fathers) and single-parent households (43% vs. 8%).

A Single Purpose: Welcoming Unmarried Churchgoers

by Roxanne Stone

I once fled a church service during a liturgy blessing for a newborn baby. I walked around the neighborhood for a good 20 minutes, hoping nobody looked out their windows to see me sobbing while I walked. Just the night before I'd been hit by a sense of certainty that I would never have biological children. Nearing the tail-end of my thirties, and newly single again after the end of a two-year relationship, the likelihood of conceiving a child was slipping away. The liturgy was beautiful—and I held no ill will toward the church or the family being blessed—I just couldn't stomach it that day.

Readers who are single will find this familiar.

That pang of loneliness as you sit alone in a church service, surrounded by couples and families. The unwelcome jab of envy when you hear about a newly engaged couple during a social hour after church. The inward eye-roll when couples are invited to sign up for the upcoming "marriage retreat" or "pre-marital seminar" during announcements.

"Is there a place for me here?" single people may ask, when getting married and starting a family are celebrated regularly from the pulpit.

And so I ask: Is there a place to talk about singleness in a report dedicated to studying households of faith?

There must be. After all, single people likely make up an increasing number in congregations. According to U.S. Census Bureau data, a record 45 percent of Americans are unmarried. And, though we don't study them in this report exploring inter-household interactions, more people than ever before are living alone (28%, as of 2016).

> "Is there a place to talk about singleness in a report dedicated to studying households of faith? There must be."

Roxanne Stone

Roxanne Stone is editor in chief at Barna Group. She is the former editorial director for *RELEVANT* magazine and has worked in publishing for more than 15 years, serving as an editor at *Christianity Today*, Group Publishing, Q Ideas and This Is Our City. She is currently working on a book examining healthy relationships between men and women in every realm of life. You can follow her on Twitter at @roxyleestone.

If churches maintain a posture that marriage is the ideal, they risk alienating a growing number of their constituents. If they uphold a nuclear family as the model household, they miss out on the richness of faith that can be intentionally nurtured in households that contain singles (not to mention households where couples have been unable to have children).

I have been a part of communities of faith that were predominantly single, as well as those that felt more "traditional," in terms of make-up: nuclear families and married couples. While I felt more seen and spoken to at the former, I also missed the interactions with married couples and children that a church community can so often offer. I believe in an integrated, multi-generational church that brings us together in various stages of life—one that celebrates and speaks into each of those stages of life. With that in mind, here are some practical offerings to better integrate single people into the life of your church family and help them intentionally nurture or participate in households of faith:

- For better and worse, a primary identifier and meaning-maker for unmarried people is their work. Talk about vocation and calling from the pulpit. Invite single people to tell their stories during services—consider, for example, a weekly or monthly moment in the service when you feature someone sharing their experience of integrating faith at work.

- Do you have any single people on staff or in your leadership? One sure way to communicate that single people have a valuable place in the life of the church is to have them represented in a visible role. In addition, having a single person in leadership will help you understand and see the needs of single people that might be different from the rest of your congregation.
- If you are a teaching pastor and are married, consider limiting the number of anecdotes in your sermon about your spouse or kids. Find stories to highlight your points that come from single people or that are more applicable no matter your listener's stage in life.
- Marriage and children are celebrated regularly from the pulpit and through various church traditions (weddings, births, baptisms). Find a way to intentionally celebrate singles from the pulpit as well, perhaps by dedicating one Sunday of the year to preach on and honor the gifts of singleness. After all, as Christians, our namesake was single, and his life is an example of the richness of faith and ministry that can result from the single life.
- Single people are, of course, not just those who have never been married. Many single people are divorced. If you know you have a number of divorced congregants, consider offering a class on healing after a divorce. Divorced people are often hurting and lonely—especially if the divorce is recent and affected their extended friend group or community. Be intentional about reaching out to divorced people and helping them feel welcome and loved by your church. An invitation to dinner can go a long way!
- Depending on your age, being single today may not be what it was like back when you were single. The dating world has changed dramatically. People are single for much longer and dating at 30 is different than dating at 20. Dating apps have

changed the game for everyone. Spend time talking to those who are single and become familiar with what their worlds look like. Dedicate sermons to the realities of trying to live chastely in this environment. Perhaps offer a class on "modern dating" that touches on topics like honor, commitment, sex and relational health.

- Loneliness for single people is real. Many single people in your congregation are probably far from family (if they moved for school or a job); they may be living alone or, as this report indicates, often with roommates, with whom they may or may not share regular routines. We are all aching for community, but for single people this can be especially acute. Help foster social activities outside Sunday services that will appeal to singles. My church in New York City did a "first Tuesday feast" modelled on the old-school potluck and everyone loved it. A church I attended in San Diego worked hard to build a community of artists and musicians and sponsored regular concerts at venues outside the church.

- Enlist older married couples or nuclear families to be "host" households. Ask them to invite single people over regularly for family dinners, game nights or even children's sporting events. Single people don't want to only be around single people—being invited into the life of a bustling family can be a source of joy, and a single person's presence can in turn be a valuable addition to an extended household.

Singleness can be a difficult time and it can be an enriching time. Your church has the opportunity to both support singles when they are struggling and empower them to flourish as a single person—whether that is only for a season or for a lifetime.

Spiritual Coaching

This study also finds evidence of intentional spiritual, even pastoral, moments in the close relationships that make up a home. Barna asked respondents about some specific examples of how some members of households and extended households not only purposefully pursue spiritual growth, but take initiative to help those around them grow as well.

Here we find that wherever grandparents, parents and spouses are present, they are steadfast in offering forms of spiritual instruction and encouragement, from setting an example to providing encouragement. Spouses are relatively less involved in instructing about traditions, perhaps because partners come to these topics on more equal footing. These are teaching moments that grandparents and parents more readily embrace, and perhaps have more natural opportunities for during respondents' upbringings. While fathers lag behind mothers in spiritual coaching overall, they are equally likely to be noted for setting an example.

Beyond the usual key figures, siblings, distant relatives and roommates seem to rarely assume spiritual coaching roles, or perhaps feel they don't have a place to. On the other hand, grandparents hardly ever participate in a household without trying to lead or interact on a spiritual level.

There is a spike among multiple relationships, particularly children, friends or other relatives, when respondents identify sources of broader encouragement. Though husbands, wives and mothers may be relationships that naturally have greater intimacy and access as advisors, community still has a valuable role to play in providing some forms of support.

Grandparents hardly ever participate in a household without trying to lead or interact on a spiritual level

Common Spiritual Coaches in All Households

How do the people in your household or extended household talk to you about their faith?

	Teaches me about the Bible	Talks with me about God's forgiveness	Sets an example	Teaches me about traditions	Encourages me to go to church	Encourages me in other ways
1	Grandparent 55%	Grandparent 56%	Grandparent 67%	Grandparent 67%	Grandparent 65%	Grandparent 62%
2	Mother 49%	Mother 52%	Mother 58%	Mother 53%	Mother 61%	Spouse 60%
3	Father 44%	Father 43%	Father 56%	Father 48%	Father 51%	Mother 57%
4	Spouse 34%	Spouse 39%	Spouse 48%	Step-parent 32%	Spouse 44%	Father 53%
5	Roommate 29%	Friend 34%	Step-parent 44%	In-laws 30%	Step-parent 41%	Friend 48%
6	Step-parent 26%	Roommate 29%	Friend 38%	Friend 26%	In-laws 41%	Step-parent 47%
7	Friend 23%	Step-parent 29%	In-laws 36%	Spouse 25%	Friend 32%	In-laws 44%
8	Unmarried partner 21%	In-laws 28%	Other relative 31%	Other non-relative 22%	Unmarried partner 29%	Unmarried partner 44%
9	Other non-relative 21%	Unmarried partner 25%	Unmarried partner 30%	Roommate 21%	Roommate 28%	Other relative 41%
10	Other relative 20%	Other relative 25%	Sibling 28%	Other relative 20%	Other relative 27%	Sibling 32%
11	In-laws 18%	Other non-relative 24%	Roommate 27%	Sibling 17%	Sibling 24%	Other non-relative 31%
12	Sibling 14%	Sibling 19%	Other non-relative 23%	Unmarried partner 16%	Other non-relative 20%	Grandchild 31%
13	Child 8%	Child 14%	Grandchild 15%	Child 7%	Child 13%	Roommate 30%
14	Grandchild 7%	Grandchild 11%	Child 13%	Grandchild 6%	Grandchild 12%	Child 26%

n=2,347 U.S. practicing Christian adults and teens, April 5–11, 2018. Respondents were only shown relationship
types they live with or who visit them regularly in their home, not including children under age 18.

Beyond the Household: Other Close Bonds

You've likely heard people describe beloved friends and neighbors as being "like family." Most practicing Christians do have some form of familial camaraderie with a non-relative. Here, the oft-larger, busier households with minors, especially single-parent households, lead the way in having more close connections beyond family members (82% vs. 74% of households without minors have at least one friend like family).

What behaviors typically distinguish such an affectionate relationship? In Barna's qualitative interviews with multiple types of households, these close bonds were shaped by a range of interactions: texting photos of pets, traveling together for vacations or big events, sharing holidays, borrowing items, providing care during illness, meeting or FaceTiming with a friend's family or helping with childcare. Sometimes the difference lay in what someone *wouldn't* do with a dear friend; for example, not feeling pressure to clean the house before the other comes over for a visit.

Households & Their Closest Friends

Do you have any people in your life who are so close they feel like family?

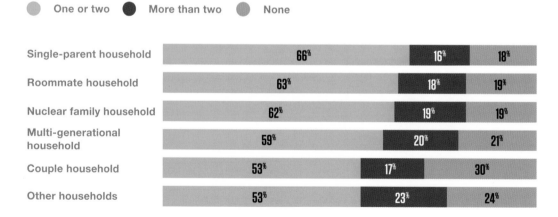

● One or two   ● More than two   ● None

	One or two	More than two	None
Single-parent household	66%	16%	18%
Roommate household	63%	18%	19%
Nuclear family household	62%	19%	19%
Multi-generational household	59%	20%	21%
Couple household	53%	17%	30%
Other households	53%	23%	24%

n≈2,347 U.S. practicing Christian adults and teens, April 5–11, 2018.

Drawing from some of the themes in the qualitative interviews, Barna's quantitative survey presented several ideas for how someone might treat their dearest friends. Respondents signal closeness with members of extended households primarily through their communication habits. Often, this means picking up the phone, either to call (55%) or text (47%). About half (48%) share holidays with these non-relatives. Merely engaging in deep conversations (46%) is another marker of this "friends like family" intimacy. Praying (42%) or having dinner together (36%) are also more common with close friends, which is telling, considering that these activities are consistent among housemate bonds in general.

Households that often welcome guests are, understandably, more likely to form intimate bonds with friends. Eighty-nine percent of practicing Christians in homes that regularly receive non-family guests can identify a friend who feels like family, compared to seven in 10 respondents in less hospitable households (71%) who have such a friendship. Across the board, welcoming households are also more likely to think of activities they share with very close friends, from having deep conversations (55% vs. 41% who don't regularly host non-family visitors) or praying together (49% vs. 38%) to sharing meals (43% vs. 31%) or borrowing items (28% vs. 16%).

Men and women seem to express closeness differently, but men are also somewhat less likely to have very close friends anyway (25% vs. 19% of women have no friends like this). It's possible they have difficulty bonding, limited social time or just have a higher bar for these "friends like family;" they are less likely than women to select any of the activities Barna suggested they might share in such a relationship. Meanwhile, women appear more communicative and connective, primarily developing their closest friendships through phone calls (60% vs. 48% of men), texts (54% vs. 39%), shared holidays (53% vs. 43%) and meaningful conversations (52% vs. 39%). We see a similar theme

Respondents signal closeness with members of extended households primarily through their communication habits

Men, Women and Expressions of Close Friendship

% of men or women who say this activity is something they would do with a non-relative they consider to be very close

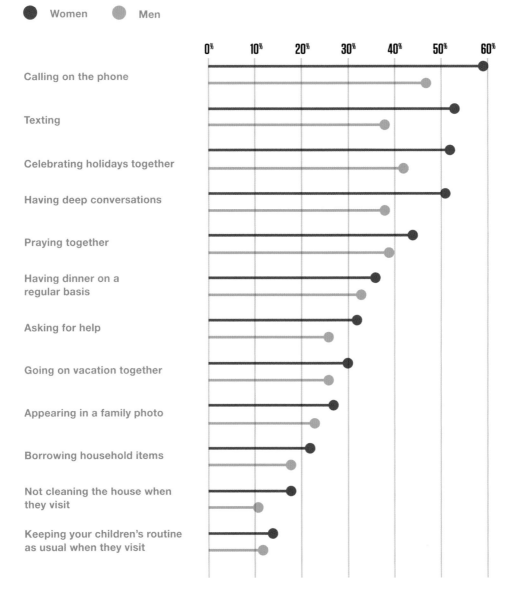

● Women   ● Men

| | 0% | 10% | 20% | 30% | 40% | 50% | 60% |

Calling on the phone

Texting

Celebrating holidays together

Having deep conversations

Praying together

Having dinner on a regular basis

Asking for help

Going on vacation together

Appearing in a family photo

Borrowing household items

Not cleaning the house when they visit

Keeping your children's routine as usual when they visit

n=2,347 U.S. practicing Christian adults and teens, April 5–11, 2018.

How Generations Interact with "Friends Like Family"

% of each generation who say this activity is something they would do with a non-relative they consider to be very close

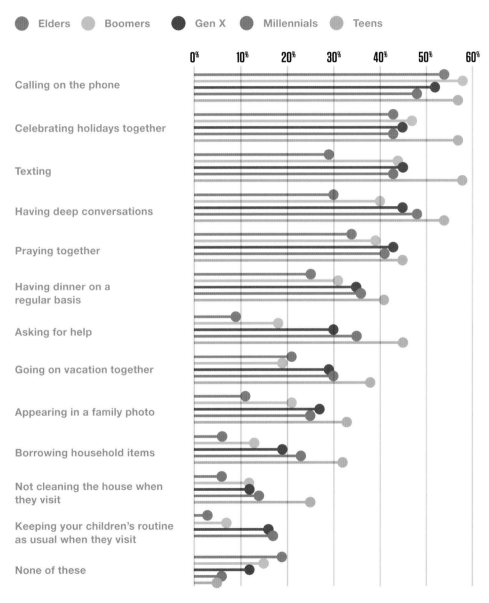

● Elders ○ Boomers ● Gen X ● Millennials ○ Teens

Calling on the phone

Celebrating holidays together

Texting

Having deep conversations

Praying together

Having dinner on a regular basis

Asking for help

Going on vacation together

Appearing in a family photo

Borrowing household items

Not cleaning the house when they visit

Keeping your children's routine as usual when they visit

None of these

n÷2,347 U.S. practicing Christian adults and teens, April 5–11, 2018.

in their willingness to confide in friends about troubles (66% vs. 51%) or have heavier conversations in which they offer sympathy (60% vs. 42%) or talk about faith (55% vs. 39%) and the Bible (51% vs. 37%). Given that we also see fathers drop off when it comes to central household activities and roles during the parenting years, it's possible that men have trouble digging into supportive relationships in general, and especially during busier times of life.

The younger a person is, the more likely he or she is to share their time, space and thoughts with friends that feel like family. Teens appear to be more creative and open than adults in these ways, though that's perhaps typical of the social lives of the middle and high school years. Millennials and Gen X are the adult generations most likely to report sharing deep chats with dear friends or depending on them for help. Boomers are apt to have phone check-ins with their closest non-relatives, but, like the couple households they often occupy, they are less likely to have such intimate friends in the first place. Whether because of health challenges, distance or generational mindsets, these responses are another peek into the solitary season that older Boomer individuals and couples find themselves in.

What About Dads?

Christian Fathers' Presence & Influence Is Lacking in Households

You might have noticed that practicing Christians in this study don't seem to share much quality time with their fathers, compared to other immediate and sometimes extended household ties. Accordingly, fathers seem to be disconnected when it comes to the actual feelings and goings-on of their housemates, namely their spouses and children. These trends become especially pronounced—and worrisome—when tracking teenagers' responses.

For all the stereotypes of teens rolling their eyes at their parents, **Gen Z in this study are actually very open with and dependent on their mothers.** Consider their descriptions of one-on-one time with other housemates, in the following chart. Today's Christian teen consistently identifies their mother as the principal housemate for almost all activities, from talking about God (70% vs. 56% fathers) to having confrontations (63% vs. 43%). Fathers only surpass mothers when it comes to playing sports (40% vs. 21%). Teenagers' siblings are equally as involved as their fathers in key spiritual interactions such as talking about God and praying together.

In the impressionable middle and high school years, even conversations about sex (41%) aren't off limits between teens and moms. (Understandably, when discussing sex, there is a bit of a difference depending on the teens' gender, with 30 percent of boys and 48 percent of girls talking about this with their mother, and 50 percent of boys and 10 percent of girls covering this topic with their father). **Mothers are teens' go-to person for all kinds of needs:** advice (78%),

Teens' One-on-One Time with Various Household Members

% of teens who say they have done this activity with this member of their household or extended household in the past month

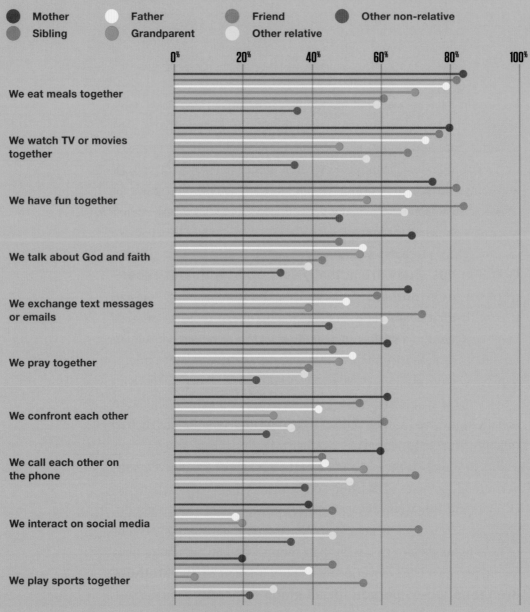

- **Mother**
- **Father**
- **Friend**
- **Other non-relative**
- **Sibling**
- **Grandparent**
- **Other relative**

We eat meals together

We watch TV or movies together

We have fun together

We talk about God and faith

We exchange text messages or emails

We pray together

We confront each other

We call each other on the phone

We interact on social media

We play sports together

n=448 U.S. practicing Christian teens, April 5–11, 2018. Respondents were only shown relationship types they live with or those who regularly visit them in their home.

encouragement (75%), sympathy (72%). Teens also primarily seek out mothers' opinions on questions of faith (72%) or the Bible (71%), as well as things that might be troubling them (78%). No wonder 68 percent of Gen Z say their mom was the one who was there for them in their last personal crisis.

Meanwhile, fathers play a somewhat key role in meeting teens' tangible needs for money (74%) and logistical help (63%), though even on these two issues, they are on par with mothers.

Realistically, we should acknowledge some factors that might push the bond between mother and child to the forefront during parenthood. If mothers spend a lot of time at home with their kids, they may become the default voice on matters practical, political, spiritual, relational and so on. Some combination of maternal or biological instinct or a traditional understanding of gender roles might also position mothers as the attentive parent with a listening ear or a greater emotional capacity. Additionally, though nuclear families are the norm for practicing Christian teens, 15 percent live in single-parent households, which more often than not are single-mother households (88% vs. 12% of teens in single-parent families who say their father lives with them).

That context granted, practicing Christian fathers still have much ground to make up. The disparity seems obvious if we assume respondents subscribe to traditional ideas that frame Christian women as having more domestic, affectionate strengths and Christian men as providers and spiritual heads of households. In such a case, fathers do not seem to be filling either the role of logistical or spiritual leader as well as mothers. If, on the other hand, respondents subscribe to an egalitarian perspective in which couples come to the business of marriage or parenting on equal footing, the gap seems even more troubling, as clearly these couples are far from parity in terms of child-rearing. The reality is that, whatever the general theology or philosophy of

Where Teens Get Support

% of teens who say they are most likely to go to this member of their household or extended household for …

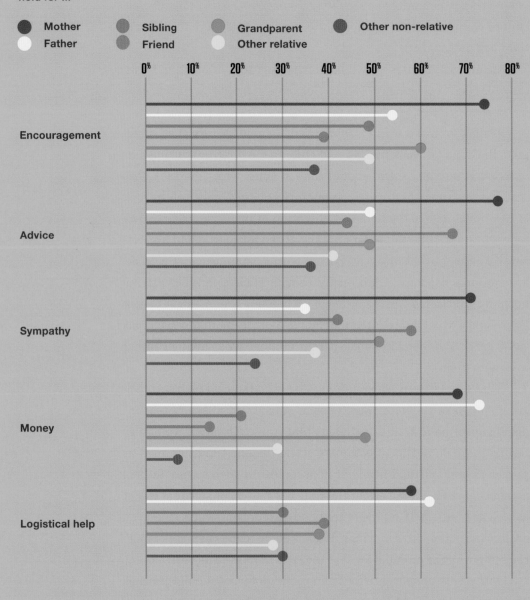

● Mother   ● Sibling   ● Grandparent   ● Other non-relative
○ Father   ● Friend   ○ Other relative

Encouragement

Advice

Sympathy

Money

Logistical help

n=448 U.S. practicing Christian teens, April 5–11, 2018. Respondents were only shown relationship types they live with or those who regularly visit them in their home.

Who Teens Talk To

% of teens who say they are most likely to talk with this member of their household or extended household about ...

● Mother ● Friend ● Grandparent ● Other non-relative
○ Father ● Sibling ○ Other relative

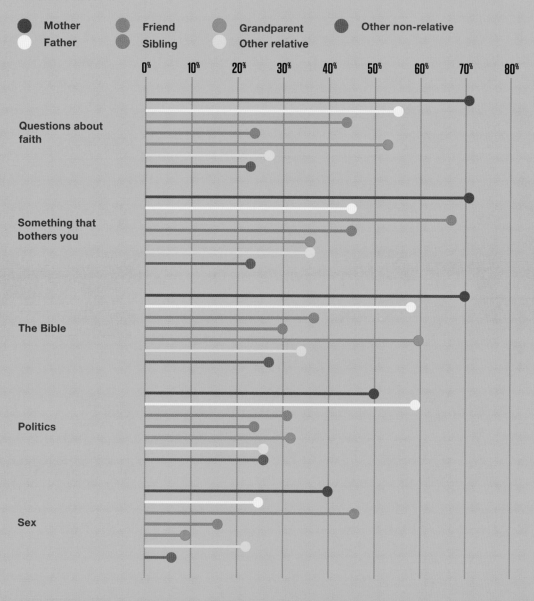

Questions about faith

Something that bothers you

The Bible

Politics

Sex

n=448 U.S. practicing Christian teens, April 5–11, 2018. Respondents were only shown relationship types they live with or those who regularly visit them in their home.

parenting, mothers consistently exceed fathers across the board, including in instilling children with the values and disciplines of their faith. Moms are simply and inarguably far ahead of dads as teens' partners in prayer (63% vs. 53%) and conversations about God (70% vs. 56%), the Bible (71% vs. 50%) or other faith questions (72% vs. 56%). This is consistent with Barna data through the years that show mothers to be the managers of faith formation (among other household routines and structures), but that doesn't make the gaps any less startling.

Additionally, at the same time that fathers and teens struggle to connect, spouses appear to become less interactive in and dependent on their own partnership when minors are in the household (as explored on page 69 and 70). This study can't say with certainty whether men and women become equally less dependent on their spouses and equally more dependent on others during this time, only that there is a redistribution of intimacy and support. Of course, a diversity of relationships and influences can be an asset to the development of an individual, a marriage or a household! But given the stark differences in how teens regard their parents, one wonders: Could a somewhat greater level of connection or at least collaboration during parenting help fathers be more engaged or impactful in their teens' lives?

After all, though mothers appear to rise to many demands of parenthood, that doesn't mean it's easy. For instance, another Barna study shows that employed Christian moms struggle not only to feel connected to their work, but also to feel a sense of "calling" at all or to find satisfaction in most areas of life.[35] Working Christian fathers, meanwhile, thrive in all of these areas. Considering that moms carry a large share of the logistical, emotional and spiritual weight at home, this contrast in parents' fulfillment is something the Church might need to help mothers and fathers address—especially as moms increasingly remain in the workplace and become breadwinners.[36] That's a dynamic Christians aren't alone in encountering: For instance, one study

Where Teens Receive Spiritual Guidance and Encouragement

% of teens who say this member of their household or extended household does the following to share about their faith

- ● Mother
- ○ Father
- ● Sibling
- ● Grandparent
- ● Friend
- ○ Other relative
- ● Other non-relative

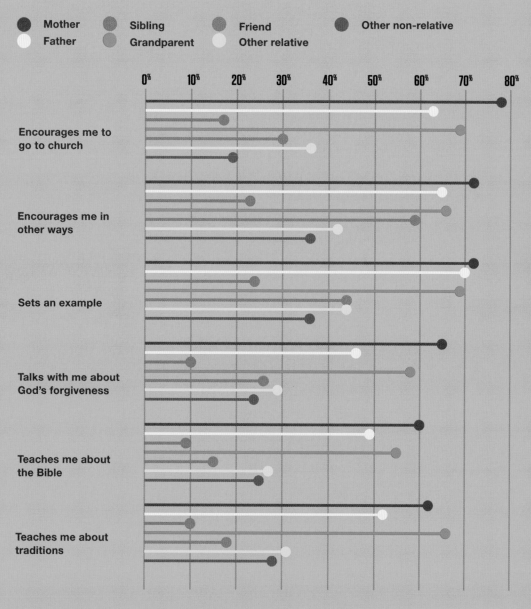

Encourages me to go to church

Encourages me in other ways

Sets an example

Talks with me about God's forgiveness

Teaches me about the Bible

Teaches me about traditions

n=327 U.S. practicing Christian teens, April 5–11, 2018. Respondents were only shown relationship types they live with or who visit them regularly in their home, not including children under age 18.

found that when wives earn a higher salary than their husbands, the latter actually does less housework.[37]

Solving this dilemma has long-term consequences for both spouse and child. As it is, when older couples who are done raising children begin to withdraw from more socially active lives, adult kids continue to esteem their moms as sources of strength, companionship and wisdom. Mothers still meet a range of needs and provide support for their grown children or, when applicable, grandchildren. Fathers, meanwhile, may find a renewed intimacy with their spouse during empty-nesting—but they don't necessarily regain an opportunity to be a crucial, impactful presence in their child's formative years and beyond. For the most part, those relationships and rituals have long been solidified—or, in some cases, those chasms between father and family may be too difficult to close. Sharing more of the challenges of raising and discipling children while they are young could help spouses, or even entire households, share more of the joys of the parent-child relationship throughout their lives.

Whatever dads do or don't intentionally invest in family faith formation, their children are still watching. For example, teens consistently identify mothers as the ones who provide spiritual guidance and instruction, with fathers well behind in encouraging church attendance (79% vs. 64%) or teaching kids about the Bible (66% vs. 50%), God's forgiveness (66% vs. 47%) and religious traditions (72% vs. 49%). Yet there is one point on which dads see a boost: Seven in 10 teens (71% vs. 73% mothers) says their dad teaches them about faith by "setting an example."

How embodied, attentive and consistent will that example be?

Equipping Parents for Spiritual Leadership

A Q&A with Barbara Reaoch

Sunday school and youth group only occur once or twice a week, and much of a child or teens' spiritual development occurs in their daily routine outside of church. What can both pastors and parents do to be better partners in discipling the next generation?

Every church needs to strategize how to support parents in their God-given responsibility to influence their families (Psalm 78:4–7). Pastors should help parents grasp the value of and need for the spiritual development of their family. By sharing preaching schedules in advance, pastors encourage their churches to commit to reading the related Bible passages. This especially helps parents prepare their families to enter more fully into worship. Churches can also promote Bible-reading, faith conversations and prayer in the home by training members to ask and discuss basic questions about the Bible passage (*What does it say? What does it mean? What does it mean to me?*) and providing simple resources based on the pastor's scripture for the sermon. As parents exercise spiritual leadership in the home, the entire family enjoys increased continuity between home and church.

What are some ways that churches can take into account the various members, schedules and needs that accom-

pany the diversity of households that likely make up their congregation?

My family currently enjoys the blessing and benefit of a multi-generational home. These are some of the special needs of this kind of household: how to encourage grandparent residents to participate in faith-based conversations with grandchildren, how to establish constructive authority boundaries, how to share responsibility in discipline issues or how to prepare for redemptive interaction in discipline issues.

In other households, needs might include: how a single parent can prioritize their own relationship with God to cope with loneliness, frustration or fear, how to prioritize the spiritual development of the family with a sole responsible adult or how to establish and maintain a relationship with a mentor.

Churches can train "family mentors" for in-home demos of faith-based conversations and redemptive discipline conversations with children and grandchildren in any type of household. For single or working parents, using Zoom, Google Hangouts, closed Facebook groups or other digital options could allow for flexibility.

When someone in a household takes on the role of spiritual coach, how can churches be there to resource and encourage them?

Churches can provide "Spiritual Leadership in the Home" classes, where parents receive practical tips for how to lead their family in Bible reading, faith-based conversations and prayer. These classes can also promote what I call a "live it and tell it" model of spiritual leadership, as described in Deuteronomy 6:6–7:

Barbara Reaoch

Director of children's division at Bible Study Fellowship

Barbara is Bible Study Fellowship's director of children's division and author of *A Jesus Christmas, Why Christmas?* and *Why Easter?* She loves God, her husband, their family and writing gospel-centered children's materials. She provides help for starting faith-based conversations and prayer at reachingheartsandminds.com.

- **Live it: Parents apply the Bible in their everyday interaction with their kids.** For example, one woman told me her kids "caught" her husband reading his Bible and then started reading their Bible too! Another woman said that when her family got home from church after hearing a sermon on Matthew 6:14-15, God gave her an opportunity to ask her son's forgiveness for speaking harshly. Later she overheard him asking his younger brother's forgiveness for an offense.

- **Tell it: Parents talk with their family about the Bible, read it and discuss how to take to heart biblical principles.** Train parents to engage their kids in "Godward conversations." For example, a Godward conversation helps a child see beyond the beauty of a sunset to the God who powerfully created it that we might know him.

Becoming Spiritually Vibrant Households

5

There are some factors in the development of our faith that are beyond our control. Namely, as chapter two covered, families of origin and personal heritage have a significant degree of influence on how a Christian is introduced to, grows in and expresses faith throughout their life. To some extent, one's location, education, resources, housemates and even community are also fixed.

This report has looked at some of these established characteristics that shape the spiritual dimensions of our lives and how they affect Christian households today—but the data frequently point to other aspects that are the product of choice.

Ultimately, rituals and relationships have a meaningful impact on faith formation and can be replicated regardless of a household's category or context. Namely, how much a household talks about faith, commits to shared spiritual disciplines or opens both heart and home to others is up to its members and leaders. The households that do all of the above have a certain vitality about them. In fact, the respondents that occupy households where these rituals are prioritized—which we'll examine in more detail below—are prone to call their home atmosphere "loving" (70%), "joyful" (60%), "playful" (50%) and "nurturing" (41%).

Barna set about grouping the households in this sample to better understand practicing Christians who are most engaged both with their faith and with others, and who seem to enjoy a warm, interactive

> Rituals and relationships have a meaningful impact on faith formation and can be replicated regardless of a household's category or context

Spiritual Vibrancy Among Practicing Christians' Households

Vibrant   Devotional   Hospitable   Dormant

Spiritual practices + spiritual conversations + hospitality

Hospitality

| 25% | 33% | 14% | 28% |

Spiritual practices + spiritual conversations

None of the above

n=2,347 U.S. practicing Christian adults and teens, April 5–11, 2018.

household environment in the process. The goal was to focus on factors that are not exclusive to a particular age or stage and indicate a commitment "to teaching and fellowship, to the breaking of bread and to prayer" (Acts 2:42, NIV). In addition, Barna wanted to understand the groups that are participating in these rituals and relationships with the most frequency. After all, in a shifting religious climate, plenty of Christians have relegated spiritual expression to their private sphere, and even the majority of nominal Christians (93%) discusses faith with housemates on at least a monthly basis. So what about the households that do so most consistently, alongside others within and beyond their home?

As stated, this study alone can't really reveal the depth of a household's spiritual interactions—but it can speak to a household's diligence in this area. So Barna created a variable that sorts respondents by frequent engagement in three markers of an actively nurtured faith:

- **Spiritual practices**—defined here as praying every day or two and reading the Bible weekly all together
- **Spiritual conversations**—defined here as talking about God and faith at least weekly all together

- **Hospitality**—defined here as welcoming non-family guests regularly, or at least several times a month

Using this stringent standard, this study presents a few possible combinations of spiritual attentiveness and community among the households of practicing Christians. Those four groups are:

- **Vibrant households**, which frequently participate in spiritual practices, spiritual conversations and hospitality.
- **Devotional households**, which frequently participate in spiritual practices and spiritual conversations, but do not often welcome non-family guests (a third, however, reports that relatives visit).
- **Hospitable households**, which frequently host non-family visitors. When it comes to spiritual practices or spiritual conversations, this group participates in just one or neither activity.
- **Dormant households**, which participate in none of these activities on a frequent basis. Some of these households engage in spiritual practices or spiritual conversations, though only occasionally. A third (35%) receives visits from family members.

A quarter of respondents in this study (25%) describes a household environment that is Vibrant. One-third (33%) qualifies as Devotional, a promising sign that the bulk of practicing Christians are in households that are at least mindful of spiritual growth. The community-builders in Hospitable households make up the smallest group (14%). Just over a quarter (28%) is Dormant, and may need the biggest push from church leaders to plug into relationships and rituals—or could benefit from the examples or outreach of other Vibrant, Devotional and Hospitable households.

Spiritual Vibrancy & Home Atmospheres

When asked to choose adjectives to describe how their home feels, most respondents readily agree their homes feel loving, comfortable, safe and joyful. However, true discrepancies emerge between Vibrant and Dormant households—even, or especially, in these areas.

Loving	70%
Comfortable	69%
Safe	67%
Joyful	60%
Peaceful	55%
Playful	50%
Casual	46%
Nurturing	41%
Intellectual	26%
Old-fashioned	23%
Artistic	19%
Messy	15%
Tense	9%
Crowded	9%
Secretive	7%
Sad	4%
In Crisis	4%

Vibrant

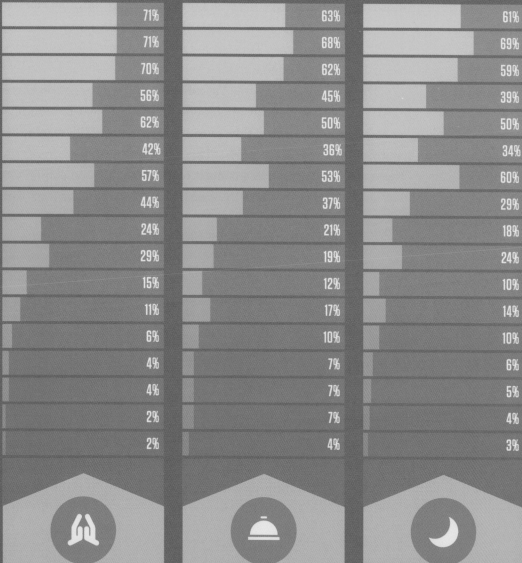

Devotional	Hospitable	Dormant
71%	63%	61%
71%	68%	69%
70%	62%	59%
56%	45%	39%
62%	50%	50%
42%	36%	34%
57%	53%	60%
44%	37%	29%
24%	21%	18%
29%	19%	24%
15%	12%	10%
11%	17%	14%
6%	10%	10%
4%	7%	6%
4%	7%	5%
2%	7%	4%
2%	4%	3%

Devotional   **Hospitable**   **Dormant**

n=2,347 U.S. practicing Christian adult and teens, April 5-11, 2018.

Profiles & Patterns Related to Vibrancy

Factors like ethnicity, location and faith history do not produce significant differences among spiritually Vibrant, Devotional, Hospitable and Dormant groups, suggesting that, for the most part, spiritual vibrancy is not determined by unchangeable characteristics, but by things any Christian can improve. This is good news for church leaders and for the households that make up their congregations.

There are, however, some logical trends related to age and household type. For instance, Hospitable environments tend to be roommate situations (18%), and are thus most represented by Millennial (35%) and Gen X respondents (30%). This is understandable, considering those in this age group and context tend to lean a lot on community, but don't necessarily share the same faith background or even daily

Household Types Broken Down by Spiritual Vibrancy

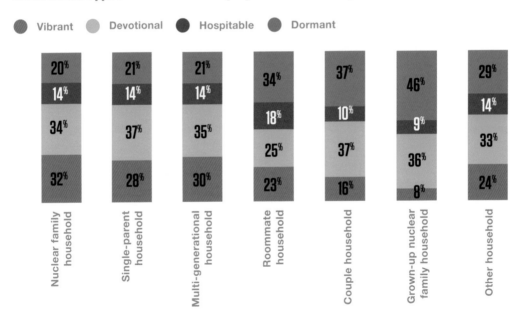

● Vibrant ● Devotional ● Hospitable ● Dormant

	Nuclear family household	Single-parent household	Multi-generational household	Roommate household	Couple household	Grown-up nuclear family household	Other household
Hospitable	20%	21%	21%	34%	37%	46%	29%
	14%	14%	14%	18%	10%	9%	14%
Devotional	34%	37%	35%	25%	37%	36%	33%
Vibrant	32%	28%	30%	23%	16%	8%	24%

n=2,347 U.S. practicing Christian adults and teens, April 5–11, 2018.

routines as their housemates. Nearly half of the respondents who live in a spiritually Dormant home are Boomers (34%) and Elders (12%), so this category sees more couples-only residences (19%), an atmosphere that, though peaceful, is much less interactive. Spiritually Vibrant homes are those typically described by Millennial (35%) and Gen X (30%) respondents, and accordingly show a significant proportion of nuclear families (33%). Single-parent, roommate households and multi-generational households (14% each) are also somewhat more common in the Vibrant segment. The most obvious common denominator here is children, which is fitting considering the data repeatedly show that the presence of minors may augment spiritual attention and community activity. Devotional environments are relatively evenly dispersed across generations and household types, perhaps capturing a middle ground for all practicing Christians.

As you can see, though this segmentation of spiritual engagement organizes households by their decisions and activities rather than their makeup, some living arrangements and stages of life perhaps more naturally come by these enriching habits. This could be due to having more members, input, community and opportunities for interaction—but that's not to say more crowded, younger or, frankly, louder households are somehow better. These habits are not exclusive to larger households or those with children; they can be cultivated in all household situations. Consider that the models of Vibrant and Devotional homes, though defined by their spiritual behaviors as a household, are also highly involved in other spiritual practices unrelated to their household context, like reading the Bible on one's own (76% and 67%, respectively) or attending small groups (51% and 48%, respectively) each week.

What Makes for a Vibrant Household?

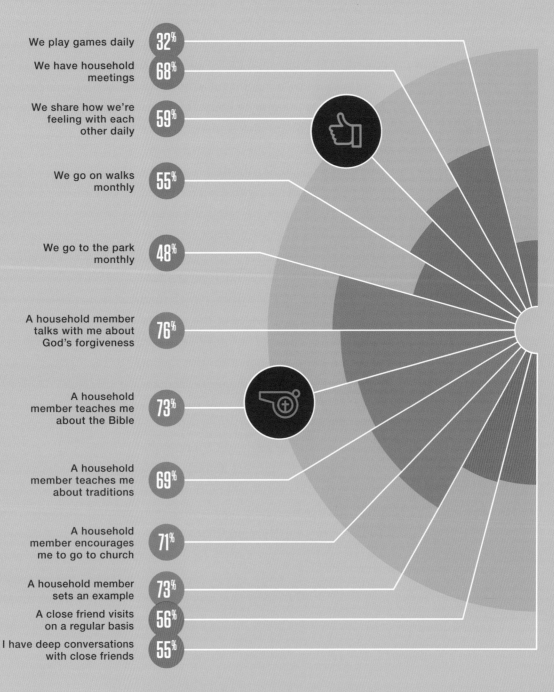

We play games daily — 32%

We have household meetings — 68%

We share how we're feeling with each other daily — 59%

We go on walks monthly — 55%

We go to the park monthly — 48%

A household member talks with me about God's forgiveness — 76%

A household member teaches me about the Bible — 73%

A household member teaches me about traditions — 69%

A household member encourages me to go to church — 71%

A household member sets an example — 73%

A close friend visits on a regular basis — 56%

I have deep conversations with close friends — 55%

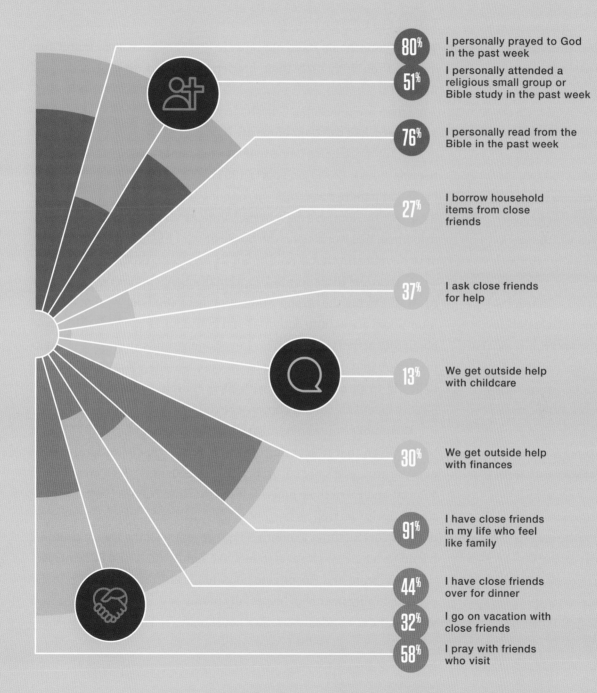

- Spends fun, quality time together
- A spiritual coach is present
- Welcomes others
- Asks for help
- Members have a personal spirituality

80% I personally prayed to God in the past week

51% I personally attended a religious small group or Bible study in the past week

76% I personally read from the Bible in the past week

27% I borrow household items from close friends

37% I ask close friends for help

13% We get outside help with childcare

30% We get outside help with finances

91% I have close friends in my life who feel like family

44% I have close friends over for dinner

32% I go on vacation with close friends

58% I pray with friends who visit

The Vibrant Way of Life

Let's Get Together

Vibrant households stand out most in that they have meaningful, fun, quality time with both their housemates and extended household members.

These are practicing Christians who know the meaning of play—and indeed, half call their home life "playful." Every day or so, members of Vibrant households come together for games (32%), singing (31%), reading books (26%) or sports (23%). They share meals (63% eat breakfast together and 75% eat dinner together) as well as their feelings (59%) on almost a daily basis. Vibrancy also correlates with group discipline, like working on the house or yard together (34% every day or two) or hosting household or family meetings (68%).

On many of these points, Devotional households are not far behind, re-emphasizing the strong connection between housemates who are intentional about faith activities and housemates who are intentional about *any* activity. And though Devotional groups stop short of inviting others into their households, they are like the Vibrant in choosing to go out to gather regularly with their church community (84% and 83%, respectively, attend church weekly).

Hospitable households align closely with other spiritually Vibrant traits. Given that welcoming others is part of the definition for each of these groups, it's not surprising that friendships play a great role in Vibrant and Hospitable households, with close friends (56% and 58%, respectively), as well as neighbors (28% and 26%, respectively) coming over several times a month. These groups lead the way in claiming friends who are so close as to feel like family (91% and 86%, respectively). Vibrant and Hospitable households are also more likely to depend on family members (especially moms or grandmothers) for help with finances, childcare or other household needs. Additionally, these

> Vibrant households stand out most in that they have meaningful, fun, quality time

Togetherness, Play and Spiritual Vibrancy

● Vibrant   ● Devotional   ● Hospitable   ● Dormant

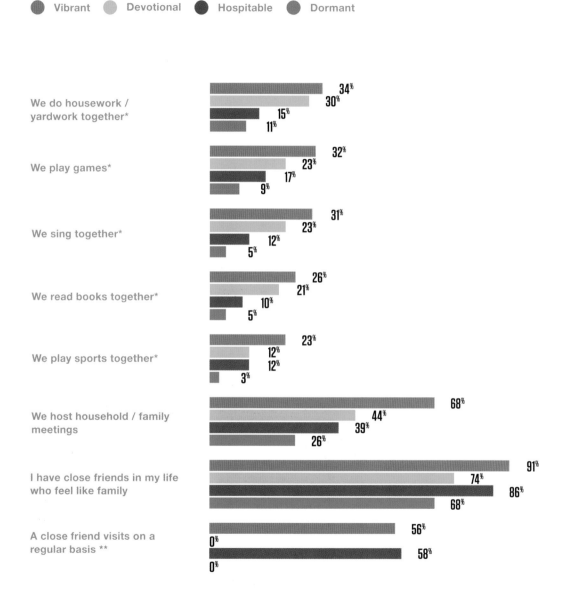

We do housework /
yardwork together*
- 34%
- 30%
- 15%
- 11%

We play games*
- 32%
- 23%
- 17%
- 9%

We sing together*
- 31%
- 23%
- 12%
- 5%

We read books together*
- 26%
- 21%
- 10%
- 5%

We play sports together*
- 23%
- 12%
- 12%
- 3%

We host household / family
meetings
- 68%
- 44%
- 39%
- 26%

I have close friends in my life
who feel like family
- 91%
- 74%
- 86%
- 68%

A close friend visits on a
regular basis **
- 56%
- 0%
- 58%
- 0%

n=2,347 U.S. practicing Christian adults and teens, April 5–11, 2018.

*% participates in these activities "all together" every day or two.

** Devotional and Dormant households are partly defined by not receiving frequent non-family guests.

Vibrant Households More Likely to Lean on Others

Do you depend on family members who do not live in your home to help with finances, childcare or other things to keep your household running?

● Vibrant ● Devotional ● Hospitable ● Dormant

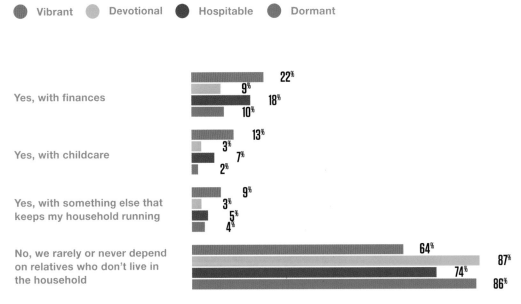

Yes, with finances
22%
9%
18%
10%

Yes, with childcare
13%
3%
7%
2%

Yes, with something else that keeps my household running
9%
3%
5%
4%

No, we rarely or never depend on relatives who don't live in the household
64%
87%
74%
86%

n≈1,899 U.S. practicing Christian adults, April 5–11, 2018.

% indicates having any household relationship that they are likely to go to for...

Advice
96%
86%
91%
76%

Sympathy
91%
81%
80%
69%

Encouragement
90%
86%
89%
74%

Logistical help
88%
76%
81%
66%

n=2,347 U.S. practicing Christian adult and teens, April 5–11, 2018.

households are quicker to name either family or non-family members they go to for advice or encouragement. Because of the way these more social households are determined, there is a natural skew toward having help—but there's also the implication that outside influences and visitors add value to a household. The Devotional and Dormant households, meanwhile, appear to be more self-sufficient, rarely if ever looking to family members outside the home for assistance.

There are important lessons for the Church in examining the ways that spiritually Vibrant households do or do not overlap with others. Namely, good things happen when those who share a home also share everyday liturgies with one another. Good things happen when those who share a home habitually share their lives with others. And all of these good things—a support system, shared regimens, recreational and creative time, spiritual discipline—are amplified when both Christian devotion and hospitality become part of the ethos of a household.

Spiritual Coaching Correlates with Vibrancy

Regardless of their level of spiritual vibrancy, households are not significantly different when it comes to their beliefs in the accuracy of the Bible, a responsibility to share their faith, a traditional view of God or a personal commitment to Jesus. This suggests that a common doctrine or theology, on its own, doesn't wholly shape and improve a Christian's lifestyle or household. In other words, someone can have "right thinking" on their own and still withhold hospitality, neglect disciplines of the faith or fail to include those who are close to them in their spiritual lives.

Instead, members of Vibrant households learn positive spiritual lessons and behaviors together through intentional, reverent moments between household members. Spiritual coaches are remarkably consistent in Vibrant homes. Among this group's distinguishing traits is the presence of someone who shares about God's forgiveness (76% vs. 59% Devotional, 49% Hospitable and 32% Dormant), the Bible (73% vs. 53% Devotional, 38% Hospitable and 27% Dormant) or traditions (69% vs. 43% Devotional, 48% Hospitable and 29% Dormant). More than six in 10 have a household member who sets a spiritual example (73% vs. 58% Devotional, 57% Hospitable and 48% Dormant)

Models of Faith & Spiritual Vibrancy

% indicates having a member of their household who does the following to share about their faith

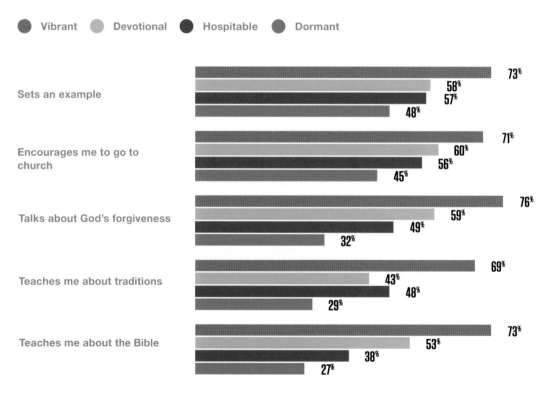

● Vibrant ● Devotional ● Hospitable ● Dormant

Sets an example
73%
58%
57%
48%

Encourages me to go to church
71%
60%
56%
45%

Talks about God's forgiveness
76%
59%
49%
32%

Teaches me about traditions
69%
43%
48%
29%

Teaches me about the Bible
73%
53%
38%
27%

n=2,347 U.S. practicing Christian adults and teens, April 5–11, 2018.

or encourages church attendance (71% vs. 60% Devotional, 56% Hospitable and 45% Dormant).

Though marriages and mothers remain central relationships when it comes to discipleship interactions, close friendships are also crucial in Vibrant households. These bonds rank closely in setting strong examples; engaging in discussions about God's forgiveness, the Bible or traditions; or commending church attendance. This syncs with other signs that friendship plays a big part in Vibrant households, and it is yet another clue as to the ways community completes a household of faith.

Within that community, and always at the periphery of this study, is the local church. We know that the practicing Christians in this sample are regularly in worship services, often with other household members. We'll conclude this report by discussing: How do pastors and leaders best promote spiritual vibrancy? How can the Church as a whole better disciple individuals toward a faithful lifestyle of togetherness, intentionality and hospitality?

Tips for Setting Up Your Home for Vibrancy

Before Barna conducted its quantitative survey of practicing Christians, we interviewed members of several highly active Christian households. Nuclear, multi-generational, single-parent and roommate contexts were represented. These in-depth, personal conversations not only helped inform the quantitative questionnaire, but provided practical tips and insights for building relationships and growing in faith as a household. Below are some recommendations and principles inspired by these individuals' routines.

- Pick a night for a weekly themed gathering, perhaps rotating hosting duties with other households. The people Barna spoke to mentioned supper clubs, game nights, "Crockpot Nights" and more.

- In roommate households, or in homes where a boarder, nanny, au pair or other live-in caretaker or guest is present, housemates might need to make an effort up front to get to know one another's backgrounds. FaceTiming with relatives, being a "plus one" for work parties or events or taking interest in others' hobbies or side hustles are some ways to share more than just the utilities bill.

- Get a kid-friendly Bible or devotional for a child, with the intent of having them read it *with* an adult, not just by themselves. One interviewee described being able to have meaningful, cross-generational conversations about the text, as well as learning from familiar stories through a new lens.

- Sit down with your housemates to discuss if you'd like to make yourselves available not only to those who naturally come into your inner circle through work, school or family but to other individuals who could use your company or even a roof over their heads. Consider whether your home might make a warm temporary residence for visiting missionaries, a host home for refugees or a safe space for foster children.

- Use a "speaking baton" (or other object) to direct family or household conversation at the dinner table. Whoever is presently holding the baton gets to share uninterrupted about their day, feelings, praise reports, interests or concerns. One parent told Barna this has been especially helpful with younger or quieter members of the household, ensuring everyone has a chance to be heard and respected.

- One way to communicate the value of certain routines and disciplines is to not throw them out when guests come over. By inviting members of an extended household to also participate in activities like cleaning the kitchen, finishing homework or saying evening prayers, you communicate that these are not rigid chores done in private but valued rituals meant to be celebrated and shared.

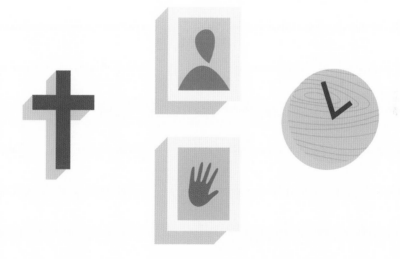

Conclusion

Leading Households of Faith

If you're a pastor or church leader, you know that even your most devoted attendees are *not* in your church most of the time. That can feel like an obstacle: How does a ministry effectively influence the daily spiritual lives of the households and families it serves—which likely represent an array of generations, backgrounds, living arrangements and routines?

We hope the data contained in this report has mitigated some of the mystery or frustration that might surround your efforts to speak with specificity into the everyday hours and relationships of your parishioners. Perhaps it has been helpful in prompting you to reexamine your own household structure and daily routine, as well as their interplay with your faith. At the very least, we offer this report as a reminder that your work in supporting Christians as they function, even thrive, throughout the week is not only within the purview of your ministry, but crucial to discipleship and the health and longevity of the Church.

A household of faith can exist anywhere, regardless of someone's history or current context, and, for the most part, it hinges on togetherness and shared opportunities for spiritual growth. The local church, a family of its own, can lead the way here. It should go without saying that means pastors, staff members and lay leaders should take the principles of spiritual vibrancy seriously and personally in their own homes. But churches must also emphasize the importance of hospitality and spiritual practices throughout their offerings—in sermons,

> Your work in supporting Christians as they function, even thrive, throughout the week is not only within the purview of your ministry, but crucial to discipleship

songs, small groups, team meetings, summer camps, Bible studies, outreach events and so on.

In this conclusion, we'll reflect on some of the lessons of this report and how they might inform your ministry to better connect and strengthen the households in your congregation.

Build—or Rebuild—Your Ministry with a Multi-Household Mindset

This study illustrates the mix of household types within the U.S. Church as a whole. Depending on your community's location or demographics, this household variety may or may not exist, but it's worth familiarizing yourself with the living arrangements that make up your congregation and determining which households your ministry could better disciple—or attract for the first time. It might be helpful to begin with reviewing member records or surveying the congregation with the goal of learning about the home lives and housemates of churchgoers. While it may appear that some environments or stages of life more naturally accompany church involvement, it's possible these are simply the arrangements to which churches have most catered. Knowing each household has different needs, ask pointed questions about how you've set up your ministries, such as:

- Does the structure of services or groups for families and children feel accessible to both fathers *and* mothers? Would participation in these same areas of ministry feel like a help or hindrance for single parents who are already carrying a heavy load? Have you made assumptions about the schedules of working dads or moms that may no longer be realistic?
- Who in your church might have a hard time making it to services—older adults with health challenges? Childless couples

who feel less engaged than families with minors? Single adults without an obvious partner or mentor who might encourage attendance? Busy nuclear or multi-generational households who could feel daunted by the Sunday morning routine? Set up carpools, volunteer teams or community groups that create a sense of accountability and camaraderie by strategically connecting younger families, single adults and elders.

- How is your church supporting households as they evolve or change categories, for any number of reasons: marriage, divorce, illness, death, a child being born or leaving home, a move into retirement or assisted living? Think about how lay leaders or other church members could mentor or check in with families in transition, especially when the spiritual coach of the home might be greatly affected by a shift or crisis.

Use Age-Specific Ministries in Service of a Household-Inclusive Church

Does your church always separate generations for teaching, worship and fellowship because it's the best route, or because it's what has been done before? Certainly, dividing by age groups is sometimes the most convenient or appropriate option for everyone involved, but it can also prevent the inter-household introductions that, this study conveys, sustain the church and boost spiritual vibrancy at home.

The data indicates the presence of kids advances spiritual conversation and practice, but most Americans will spend the majority of their lives without minors in their households. Thus, there could be spiritual and social value for both old and young, parents and non-parents, in welcoming the involvement of kids and teens in main services or small groups, at least occasionally. Allowing all attendees to have church engagement of a similar nature could also eliminate a sense that a certain household type is prioritized in the activities of the church.

Finally, early and thoughtful inclusion of young attendees could ease some of the alienation or disillusionment that teens may encounter as they "graduate" from a siloed child or youth ministry and become single young adults, only to struggle to feel well-connected to their local church or to seasoned mentors who could help them navigate college, career, relationships and faith questions. One global study of teens, conducted by OneHope, points to three main things that most strengthen the faith of youth: positive family experience, engagement in religious texts and involvement in a faith community. The local church, working alongside households, can speak to all of the above and help transmit enduring faith to the next generation.[38]

Coach Christians in Ways Their Upbringing Did Not

Christians who didn't grow up in a household of faith (or at least not one that provided a positive example) may need help understanding and establishing meaningful rituals. Conversely, Christians whose faith has strong roots in their upbringing may almost instinctively participate in the community and rituals of the Church, yet need some help scrutinizing the reasons behind their worldview or lifestyle.

Though the traditions or terminology will undoubtedly vary by denomination, any church can benefit from an annual or ongoing effort to delve into topics like hymns, sacraments, the liturgical calendar, spiritual gifts, missiology, the writers of the Gospels or the history of various Christian movements. If religion or theology professors attend your church, see if they might be willing to share a reading list or invite a church book club to shadow a lecture. Give even the "no-brainers" of practicing Christianity a careful, thorough explanation; for example, a class or series could focus on everyday disciplines, like how to pray or read the Bible, or regular church rituals, like tithing or baptisms.

How these classes or groups are presented to the congregation is just as important as what is covered in them. Some might guess these are opportunities for new believers to learn about the faith, so you might want to explicitly state when these are also moments for established members of your church to meet recent attendees, or for life-long Christians to wrestle with the complexities of their beliefs and feel permission to say, "I've never thought about this before." Consider making these classes open to all ages or perhaps to have parallel groups for adults and kids, to educate the whole church at once and provide entire families with chances for further conversation or application.

Make an Impact by Making Memories

Practicing Christians' reports of household interactions show that spiritual practices are prioritized when all types of activities are common: games, house projects, heart-to-heart talks, reading, singing … The list goes on. What's more, a correlation between hospitality and faithfulness speaks to the power of lively extended households consisting of both family and non-family.

Ministries have a duty to help their members understand all of life as worship, as well as to emphasize closeness, collaboration and fun as signs of life in the church. It shouldn't be hard for Christians to identify the ways in which their local church pushes them not only to know God but also to know their brothers and sisters in Christ, perhaps through dinner clubs, church-wide events, hobby groups, open mic nights and more. These could be chances for churches to welcome members as well as visitors, the broader community and those in need. Pastors may need to be bold (and humble) enough to acknowledge when faith formation is best aided not by services and sermons alone but by play and friendship.

Of course, even when churches communicate openness, joy and hospitality, some individuals and households may have trouble

> Pastors may need to be bold (and humble) enough to acknowledge when faith formation is best aided not by services and sermons alone but by play and friendship

applying these values. Sometimes this is an issue of temperament or intention, but fulfilling the role of host or visitor can also be made difficult by distance, a sensitive housemate relationship, transportation troubles, compromised health or simply a diminished community. Think about ways to formalize or incentivize opportunities for attendees of all age groups and households to gather inside and outside of services—to both extend *and* receive hospitality. Sometimes this neighborliness looks like hosting others, but it could also require offering help or paying a visit. This generosity speaks to a range of pain points mentioned in this report: single parents who need child care, roommates who lack mentors, elderly who are lonely, ill or otherwise isolated. It also brings old and young together and creates an image of the Church as one big, diverse "extended household."

Don't forget that you, as a church leader, are a part of that picture as well. For churchgoers, having a more personal and intimate experience of their pastor as personal shepherd could go a long way in modeling hospitality and openness. It might be time for pastors and other leaders, elders or staff members to revive the somewhat lost tradition of "house calls." Consider making it a weekly or biweekly ritual to have dinner, coffee or dessert at parishioners' houses. Or, if that isn't easily arranged in a large congregation, invite groups of parishioners to have dinner at leaders' homes.

In summarizing the recommendations that stem from this research, perhaps we can do no better than Romans 12, which begins with its famous exhortation to be "a living and holy sacrifice." As the chapter goes on, the focus shifts from the individual to the collective— from "your bodies" to "Christ's body." We are reminded, "We all belong to each other." "Love each other with genuine affection." "Work hard and serve the Lord enthusiastically." "Keep on praying." "Don't be too proud to enjoy the company of ordinary people." "Always be eager to practice hospitality." Taken together, these principles build not only a vibrant household but a flourishing community of faith.

Household Profiles

A

The following pages offer an overview of the primary households that Barna categorized and analyzed in this report, including their:

- Demographics
- Extended households
- Levels of spiritual vibrancy
- Weekly faith engagement
- Shared activities

These fact sheets are based on the responses of U.S. practicing Christians who do not live alone and describe living in these types of households.

Nuclear Family Households

- Include two parents and their child(ren), with at least one minor in the home
- Make up 25 percent of U.S. practicing Christians who do not live alone

Demographics

Generations

- Gen Z, 49%
- Millennials, 18%
- Gen X, 30%
- Boomers, 2%

Ethnicity

- White, 69%
- Black, 11%
- Hispanic, 13%
- Asian, 4%
- Other, 3%

Location

- Urban, 34%
- Suburban, 40%
- Rural, 16%
- Small town, 10%

Household Income

- < $60K, 36%
- $60–90K, 36%
- $100K+, 28%

Spiritual Vibrancy Levels

- Vibrant
- Hospitable
- Devotional
- Dormant

| 32% | 34% | 14% | 20% |

Respondents' Weekly Faith Engagement

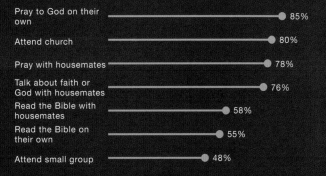

- Pray to God on their own — 85%
- Attend church — 80%
- Pray with housemates — 78%
- Talk about faith or God with housemates — 76%
- Read the Bible with housemates — 58%
- Read the Bible on their own — 55%
- Attend small group — 48%

Hospitality
Frequent guests include:

- Close friend (26%)
- Brother or sister (15%)
- Mother (14%)
- Grandparent (13%)
- Neighbor (10%)
- Spouse's mother or father (10%)

Eight in 10 (81%) have a close friend who feels like family.

More than a third (36%) says they do not receive guests on a regular basis.

Commonly Shared Household Activities

% say this is something they do all together every day or two

- Eat dinner — 75%
- Eat breakfast — 54%
- Watch TV / movies — 53%
- Share feelings — 48%
- Do housework / yardwork — 25%
- Play games — 24%
- Sing — 23%
- Read books — 21%
- Play sports — 17%
- House projects — 12%

Single-Parent Households

- Include one parent and their child(ren)
- Make up 12 percent of U.S. practicing Christians who do not live alone

Demographics

Generations

- Gen Z, 22%
- Millennials, 23%
- Gen X, 29%
- Boomers, 20%
- Elders, 5%

Ethnicity

- White, 48%
- Black, 29%
- Hispanic, 15%
- Asian, 2%
- Other, 4%

Location

- Urban, 30%
- Suburban, 40%
- Rural, 18%
- Small town, 12%

Household Income

- < $60K, 74%
- $60–90K, 18%
- $100K+, 8%

Hospitality

Frequent guests include:

- Close friend (25%)
- Brother or sister (19%)
- Mother (14%)
- Neighbor (12%)
- Other relative (11%)
- Child's close friend (11%)

Eight in 10 (82%) have a close friend who feels like family.

More than a third (35%) says they do not receive guests on a regular basis.

Spiritual Vibrancy Levels

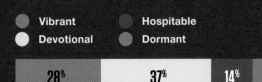

- Vibrant
- Devotional
- Hospitable
- Dormant

| 28% | 37% | 14% | 21% |

Respondents' Weekly Faith Engagement

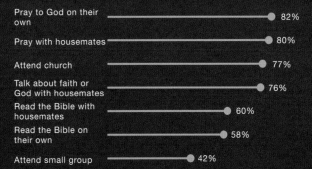

- Pray to God on their own — 82%
- Pray with housemates — 80%
- Attend church — 77%
- Talk about faith or God with housemates — 76%
- Read the Bible with housemates — 60%
- Read the Bible on their own — 58%
- Attend small group — 42%

Commonly Shared Household Activities

% say this is something they do all together every day or two

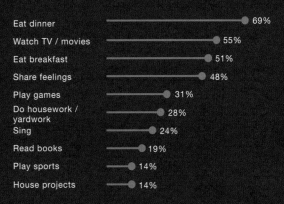

- Eat dinner — 69%
- Watch TV / movies — 55%
- Eat breakfast — 51%
- Share feelings — 48%
- Play games — 31%
- Do housework / yardwork — 28%
- Sing — 24%
- Read books — 19%
- Play sports — 14%
- House projects — 14%

Multi-Generational Households

- Include at least three generations in the home, or a grandparent raising a grandchild
- Make up 12 percent of U.S. practicing Christians who do not live alone

Demographics

Generations

- Gen Z, 14%
- Millennials, 27%
- Gen X, 28%
- Boomers, 28%
- Elders, 4%

Ethnicity

- White, 60%
- Black, 21%
- Hispanic, 13%
- Asian, 3%
- Other, 3%

Location

- Urban, 35%
- Suburban, 40%
- Rural, 15%
- Small town, 10%

Household Income

- < $60K, 52%
- $60–90K, 33%
- $100K+, 15%

Spiritual Vibrancy Levels

- Vibrant
- Devotional
- Hospitable
- Dormant

| 30% | 35% | 14% | 21% |

Respondents' Weekly Faith Engagement

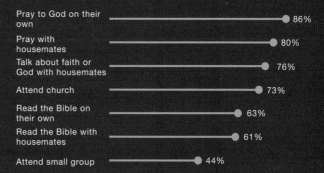

- Pray to God on their own — 86%
- Pray with housemates — 80%
- Talk about faith or God with housemates — 76%
- Attend church — 73%
- Read the Bible on their own — 63%
- Read the Bible with housemates — 61%
- Attend small group — 44%

Hospitality

Frequent guests include:

- Close friend (25%)
- Brother or sister (17%)
- Neighbor (17%)
- Other relative (11%)
- Grandchild (10%)
- Grown children (9%)

Almost eight in 10 (79%) have a close friend who feels like family.

One-third (33%) says they do not receive guests on a regular basis.

Commonly Shared Household Activities

% say this is something they do all together every day or two

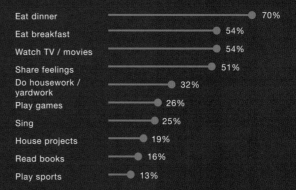

- Eat dinner — 70%
- Eat breakfast — 54%
- Watch TV / movies — 54%
- Share feelings — 51%
- Do housework / yardwork — 32%
- Play games — 26%
- Sing — 25%
- House projects — 19%
- Read books — 16%
- Play sports — 13%

Roommate Households

- Include roommates, boarders, siblings, other non-relatives or other relatives (excluding parents, grandparents or grandchildren)
- Make up 17 percent of U.S. practicing Christians who do not live alone

Demographics

Generations

- Gen Z, 6%
- Millennials, 39%
- Gen X, 20%
- Boomers, 27%
- Elders, 7%

Ethnicity

- White, 53%
- Black, 26%
- Hispanic, 16%
- Asian, 2%
- Other, 3%

Location

- Urban, 32%
- Suburban, 40%
- Rural, 16%
- Small town, 11%

Household Income

- < $60K, 75%
- $60–90K, 14%
- $100K+, 10%

Hospitality
Frequent guests include:

- Close friend (26%)
- Brother or sister (15%)
- Neighbor (11%)
- Boyfriend or girlfriend (9%)
- Other relative (8%)
- Mother (8%)

Eight in 10 (81%) have a close friend who feels like family.

Four in 10 (40%) say they do not receive guests on a regular basis.

Spiritual Vibrancy Levels

- Vibrant
- Devotional
- Hospitable
- Dormant

| 23% | 25% | 18% | 34% |

Respondents' Weekly Faith Engagement

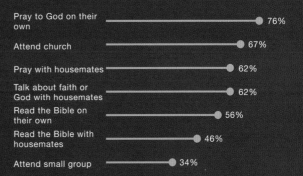

Pray to God on their own	76%
Attend church	67%
Pray with housemates	62%
Talk about faith or God with housemates	62%
Read the Bible on their own	56%
Read the Bible with housemates	46%
Attend small group	34%

Commonly Shared Household Activities

% say this is something they do all together every day or two

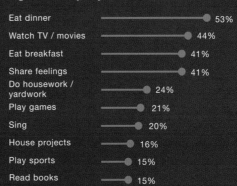

Eat dinner	53%
Watch TV / movies	44%
Eat breakfast	41%
Share feelings	41%
Do housework / yardwork	24%
Play games	21%
Sing	20%
House projects	16%
Play sports	15%
Read books	15%

Couple Households

- Include spouses only
- Make up 14 percent of U.S. practicing Christians who do not live alone

Demographics

Generations

- Millennials, 5%
- Gen X, 15%
- Boomers, 59%
- Elders, 22%

Ethnicity

- White, 86%
- Black, 5%
- Hispanic, 6%
- Asian, 1%
- Other, 1%

Location

- Urban, 25%
- Suburban, 43%
- Rural, 21%
- Small town, 12%

Household Income

- < $60K, 54%
- $60–90K, 31%
- $100K+, 15%

Hospitality
Frequent guests include:

- Grown child (29%)
- Grandchild (23%)
- Close friend (15%)
- Son-in-law or daughter-in-law (14%)
- Neighbor (10%)
- Brother or sister (10%)

Seven in 10 (70%) have a close friend who feels like family.

Half (49%) say they do not receive guests on a regular basis.

Spiritual Vibrancy Levels

- Vibrant
- Devotional
- Hospitable
- Dormant

| 16% | 37% | 10% | 37% |

Respondents' Weekly Faith Engagement

- Pray to God on their own — 94%
- Attend church — 81%
- Pray with housemates — 70%
- Talk about faith or God with housemates — 67%
- Read the Bible on their own — 56%
- Read the Bible with housemates — 50%
- Attend small group — 32%

Commonly Shared Household Activities

% say this is something they do all together every day or two

- Eat dinner — 81%
- Watch TV / movies — 65%
- Share feelings — 54%
- Eat breakfast — 53%
- Do housework / yardwork — 18%
- House projects — 9%
- Play games — 8%
- Sing — 6%
- Read books — 6%
- Play sports — 2%

Notes

B

1. Barna Group. *Spiritual Conversations in the Digital Age*. (Ventura, CA: Barna).

2. Bretz, Lauren, "As Rents Rise, More Renters Turn to Doubling Up," Zillow Research. December 14, 2017. https://www.zillow.com/research/rising-rents-more-roommates-17618/; Stepler, Renee, "Number of U.S. adults cohabiting with a partner continues to rise, especially among those 50 and older," Pew Research Center. April 6, 2017. http://www.pewresearch.org/fact-tank/2017/04/06/number-of-u-s-adults-cohabiting-with-a-partner-continues-to-rise-especially-among-those-50-and-older/; Vespa, Jonathan, "The Changing Economics and Demographics of Young Adulthood: 1975–2016," US Census Bureau. April 2017. https://www.census.gov/content/dam/Census/library/publications/2017/demo/p20-579.pdf.

3. Pinsker, Joe, "The Not-So-Great Reason Divorce Rates Are Declining," *The Atlantic*. September 25, 2018. https://www.theatlantic.com/family/archive/2018/09/millennials-divorce-baby-boomers/571282/.

4. Livingston, Gretchen, "They're Waiting Longer, but U.S. Women Today More Likely to Have Children Than a Decade Ago," Pew Research Center. January 18, 2018. http://www.pewsocialtrends.org/2018/01/18/theyre-waiting-longer-but-u-s-women-today-more-likely-to-have-children-than-a-decade-ago/.

5. Cohn, D'vera and Jeffrey S. Passel, "A record 64 million Americans live in multigenerational households," Pew Research Center. April 5, 2018. http://www.pewresearch.org/fact-tank/2018/04/05/a-record-64-million-americans-live-in-multigenerational-households/.

6. Angier, Natalie, "The Changing American Family," *The New York Times*. November 25, 2013. https://www.nytimes.com/2013/11/26/health/families.html.

7. Rampell, Catherine. "U.S. Women on the Rise as Family Breadwinner," *The New York Times*. May 29, 2013. https://www.nytimes.com/2013/05/30/business/economy/women-as-family-breadwinner-on-the-rise-study-says.html.

8. U.S. Census Bureau, "Current Population Survey – Subject Definitions," https://www.census.gov/programs-surveys/cps/technical-documentation/subject-definitions.html#household.

9. U.S. Census Bureau, "Historical Households Tables," updated November 2017. https://www.census.gov/data/tables/time-series/demo/families/households.html.

10. Barna Group, "Is Gen Z the Most Success-Oriented Generation?" June 6, 2018. https://www.barna.com/research/is-gen-z-the-most-success-oriented-generation/.

11. Barna Group, *The Generosity Gap*. (Ventura, CA: 2017) 27.

12. From a Barna study conducted for the forthcoming book *Faith for Exiles*, Baker Books, 2019.

13. Barna Group, "Atheism Doubles Among Generation Z," January 24, 2018. https://www.barna.com/research/atheism-doubles-among-generation-z/.

14. Puffer, K. A., Pence, K. G., Graverson, T. M., Wolfe, M., Pate, E., & Clegg, S. (2008). Religious Doubt and Identity Formation: Salient Predictors of Adolescent Religious Doubt. *Journal of Psychology and Theology*, 36(4), 270–284.

15. Allport, G. W. (Gordon W. (1960). *The individual and his religion : a psychological interpretation*. New York : Macmillan.

16. Puffer, et al, 2008.

17. Beck (1990) as quoted by: Puffer, K. A., Pence, K. G., Graverson, T. M., Wolfe, M., Pate, E., & Clegg, S. (2008). Religious Doubt and Identity Formation: Salient Predictors of Adolescent Religious Doubt. *Journal of Psychology and Theology*, 36(4), 270–284.

18. Newman, B. M., & Newman, P. R. (2017). *Development Through Life: A Psychosocial Approach* - Standalone Book (13 edition). San Fransisco, CA: Cengage Learning.

19. Newbigin, L. (1995). *Proper Confidence: Faith, Doubt, and Certainty in Christian Discipleship* (35384th edition). Grand Rapids: Eerdmans.

20. U.S. Department of Labor, Bureau of Labor Statistics, "Average hours per day spent in selected activities by employment status and sex," accessed November 2, 2018. https://www.bls.gov/charts/american-time-use/activity-by-emp.htm.

21. Cigna, "New Cigna Study Reveals Loneliness at Epidemic Levels in America," May 1, 2018. https://www.multivu.com/players/English/8294451-cigna-us-loneliness-survey/.

22. Kapp, Diana, "Does It Count as a Family Dinner if It's Over in Eight Minutes?" *Wall Street Journal.* September 17, 2013. https://www.wsj.com/articles/does-it-a-family-dinner-if-its-over-in-eight-minutes-1379458810.

23. Barna Group, *Spiritual Conversations,* 75.

24. Barna Group, "Generous People Are Rarely Single-Issue Donors," October 16, 2018. https://www.barna.com/research/generosity-infographic/.

25. Barna Group, *Christians at Work.* (Ventura, CA: 2018) 90.

26. Barna Group, *Spiritual Conversations*, 62.

27. Crouch, Andy, *The Tech-Wise Family.* Ada, MI: Baker Books, 2017.

28. Vespa, "Changing Economics and Demographics of Young Adulthood."

29. Vespa, "Changing Economics and Demographics of Young Adulthood."

30. Volpe, Allie, "The Strange, Unique Intimacy of the Roommate Relationship," *The Atlantic.* August 13, 2018. https://www.theatlantic.com/family/archive/2018/08/the-strange-unique-intimacy-of-the-roommate-relationship/567296/.

31. Weale, Sally, "Boomerang offspring damage parents' wellbeing, study finds," *The Guardian.* March 7, 2018. https://www.theguardian.com/society/2018/mar/07/boomerang-offspring-damage-parents-wellbeing-study-finds; Weale, Sally, "Boomerang children can be good for family relationships – study," *The Guardian.* June 29, 2018. https://www.theguardian.com/education/2018/jun/29/boomerang-children-can-be-good-for-family-relationships-study.

32. Coontz, Stephanie, *The Way We Never Were: American Families and the Nostalgia Trap.* New York: Basic Books, 1993.

33. DiPrete, Thomas A. et al., "Segregation in Social Networks Based on Acquaintanceship and Trust," *American Journal of Sociology* 116, no. 4 (January 2011): 1234–83, http://www.stat.columbia.edu/~gelman/research/published/DiPreteetal.pdf.

34. Cigna, "New Cigna Study."

35. Barna Group, *Christians at Work*, 34.

36. Cooney, Samantha, "More Women Are Their Family's Sole Breadwinner Than Ever Before," *Time*. December 20, 2016. http://time.com/4607876/female-breadwinners-rise-report/; Glynee, Sarah Jane, "Breadwinning Mothers Are Increasingly the U.S. Norm," Center for American Progress. December 19, 2016. https://www.americanprogress.org/issues/women/reports/2016/12/19/295203/breadwinning-mothers-are-increasingly-the-u-s-norm/.

37. Besen-Cassino, Yasemin and Dan Cassino, "Division of House Chores and the Curious Case of Cooking: The Effects of Earning Inequality on House Chores among Dual-Earner Couples," *About Gender 3,* no. 6 (2014). https://doi.org/10.15167/2279-5057/ag.2014.3.6.176.

38. Hoskins, Bob and Robert D. Hoskins, *Attitudes & Behaviors of Youth*. Pompano Beach, FL: OneHope, 2012.

Methodology

C

This study began with in-depth qualitative interviews with highly active Christians of various household types: two nuclear families (white Millennial parents with young children), one multi-generational family (Asian American household with children and boarders), one single-parent family (African American family that is sometimes multi-generational) and a roommate household (white Millennial males). Key insights about what makes a vibrant household or how faith grows in a household setting were initially identified through this research.

The results from the qualitative interviews were used to shape the questionnaire for quantitative online surveys conducted from April 5–11, 2018. In total, 2,347 interviews were conducted, including 448 with teens between the ages of 13–17. In order to qualify, respondents had to identify as Christian, agree strongly that their faith is very important in their life today and report attending a church service at least once in the past month. The margin of error for the total sample is +/- 1.8 percentage points at the 95 percent confidence level.

Individuals living by themselves are excluded from this study. This sample is not designed to be representative of all household types in the U.S. As the goal of this study is to observe interactions among practicing Christians who live together and how faith is experienced and transmitted among them, households of a single person did not qualify for participation.

All research that seeks to capture the dynamics of a population has some inherent limitations, but is useful to observe patterns and differences that reveal insights about the surveyed group. Online panelists are a collection of people who have pre-agreed to take surveys for some compensation, which may represent some motivational biases, so our surveys include quality control measures to ensure respondents are providing truthful and thoughtful answers to questions. When Barna samples from panels, respondents are invited from a randomly selected group of the U.S. population for maximum representation. For this study, researchers set quotas to obtain a minimum reasonable sample by household composition for statistical analysis. Additionally, quotas were set by a variety of demographic factors and the data was weighted by ethnicity, education, region and gender to reflect their natural presence among the practicing Christian segment.

Glossary

Faith Segments

Practicing Christians are self-identified Christians who say their faith is very important in their lives and have attended a worship service within the past month.

Evangelical Christians meet nine criteria, which include: having made a personal commitment to Jesus Christ that is still important in their life today; believing that, when they die, they will go to heaven because they have confessed their sins and accepted Jesus Christ as their Savior; saying their faith is very important in their lives; believing they have a personal responsibility to share their religious beliefs about Christ with non-Christians; believing that Satan exists; believing that Jesus Christ lived a sinless life on earth; asserting that the

Bible is accurate in all that it teaches; believing that eternal salvation is possible only through grace, not works; and describing God as the all-knowing, all-powerful, perfect deity who created the universe and still rules it today. Being classified as an evangelical is not dependent on church attendance or denominational affiliation, and respondents are not asked to describe themselves as "evangelical."

Nominal Christians are self-identified Christians who do not indicate having a personal commitment to Jesus.

Generations

Gen Z: born between 1999 and 2015
Millennials: born between 1984 and 1998
Gen X: born between 1965 and 1983
Boomers: born between 1946 and 1964
Elders: born in 1945 or earlier

Households

Households were determined based on respondents' descriptions of their households. Practicing Christians who live alone did not qualify for participation in this study of household interactions.

Nuclear family households include two married parents and their child(ren) under the age of 18. A second type, **grown-up nuclear family households**, includes two parents who live with only their adult child(ren).

Single-parent households include an unmarried parent and their child(ren) of any age. A single-parent household may also be a multi-generational household. Single parents who live with a partner are not included in this category.

Couple households include households with married couples who do not have children or anyone else living in the home.

Multi-generational households are comprised of at least three generations in the home or a grandparent raising a grandchild. The household may also have non-family relatives living with them, such as borders or roommates, but these households do not overlap with roommate households.

Roommate households are made up of unmarried adults who share a home with a roommate or boarder.

Other households include teens or adults who live with another family member besides their parents, those who live with roommates but also live with a spouse and / or a child, or adults who live with their adult child and his or her spouse. All adults in this category do not fit into other categories defined above.

Acknowledgments

D

First, Barna Group wishes to thank our partners at Lutheran Hour Ministries, including Ashley Bayless, Kurt Buchholz, Tony Cook and Jeff Craig-Meyer, as well as their team members who participated in pivotal early workshops based on this study's findings.

We're very grateful for the insights of our expert contributors: Jason Broge, Bianca Robinson Howard, David Meggers, Sandra Maria Van Opstal and Barbara Reaoch.

The research for this study was coordinated by Brooke Hempell and Traci Hochmuth, with foundational analysis by Susan Mettes and data verification by Pam Jacob. Alyce Youngblood wrote and edited the report, with direction from Roxanne Stone. Doug Brown proofread the manuscript. Chaz Russo designed the cover and infographics, and Annette Allen designed interior layout. Brenda Usery managed production. Jennifer Hamel and Mallory Holt coordinated as project managers.

Additional thanks for the support of our Barna colleagues: Amy Brands, Daniel Copeland, Bill Denzel, Aly Hawkins, Raven Hinson, Savannah Kimberlin, David Kinnaman, Steve McBeth, Jess Villa and Todd White.

About the Project Partners

E

Barna Group is a research firm dedicated to providing actionable insights on faith and culture, with a particular focus on the Christian Church. Since 1984, Barna has conducted more than one million interviews in the course of hundreds of studies, and has become a go-to source for organizations that want to better understand a complex and changing world from a faith perspective. Barna's clients and partners include a broad range of academic institutions, churches, non-profits and businesses, such as Alpha, the Templeton Foundation, Fuller Seminary, the Bill and Melinda Gates Foundation, Maclellan Foundation, DreamWorks Animation, Focus Features, Habitat for Humanity, The Navigators, NBC-Universal, the ONE Campaign, Paramount Pictures, the Salvation Army, Walden Media, Sony and World Vision. The firm's studies are frequently quoted by major media outlets such as *The Economist*, BBC, CNN, *USA Today*, the Wall Street Journal, Fox News, *Huffington Post, The New York Times* and the *Los Angeles Times*. • **barna.com**

Lutheran Hour Ministries (LHM) is a trusted expert in global media that equips and engages a vibrant volunteer base to passionately proclaim the Gospel to more than 100 million people worldwide each week. Through its headquarters in St. Louis, Missouri, and ministry centers on six continents, LHM reaches into more than 50 countries, often bringing Christ to places where no other Christian evangelistic organizations are present. • **lhm.org**

Exploring the Digital Family Dynamic

THE TECH-WISE FAMILY

Everyday Steps for Putting Technology in Its Proper Place

MIN   MAX

ANDY CROUCH
AUTHOR OF *CULTURE MAKING*

With new insights and research from **Barna**

Provides a framework for tough questions such as:

- What are some important family values to embrace in the digital age?
- Does our use of technology move us closer to the values we've embraced?
- Are familial relationships suffering as a result of technology's distractions?
- Has "real life" taken a backseat to virtual life?

Making wise choices about technology in the context of family is more than just setting internet filters and screen-time limits for children. It's about developing wisdom, character, and courage in the way we use digital media rather than accepting technology's promises of ease, instant gratification, and the world's knowledge at our fingertips. And that's true for everyone in the family, not just the kids. Drawing on in-depth original research from Barna, Andy Crouch (leading cultural commentator and the author of *Playing God* and *Culture Making*) shows how the choices we make about technology have consequences we may never have considered. For anyone who has felt their family relationships suffer or their time slip away amid technology's distractions, this book will provide a path forward to reclaiming "real life" in a world of digital devices.

Learn more at
**barna.com/
techwise**

Go and Tell—But How?

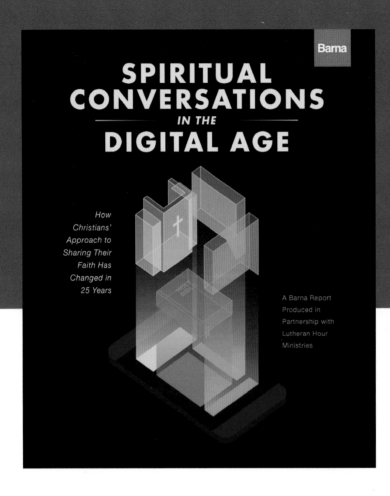

You will learn:

- How priorities and practices have shifted over the past 25 years, including the impact of social media
- Perceptions of faith sharing from both sides of the conversation—the sharer and the hearer
- A data-based profile of eager evangelists
- Generational analysis of today's climate for spiritual conversations

How is our screen-driven society changing the way people talk about their faith? What are the emotions and feelings that people experience when they have these conversations? And what can we learn from those Christians who are most active in sharing their faith with others?

This research will help churches come alongside believers and empower them with confidence to talk about their faith. In doing so, we hope to see Christians begin to make the connections between their everyday, ordinary life and the faith that sustains them. And to tell others the good news of Jesus.

Learn more at
**barna.com/
spiritualconversations**